LEARNING SKILLS FOR MANAGERS

Practical Tools and Techniques to Turbo-charge Your Career

Samuel A. Malone

Oak Tree Press
Dublin

Oak Tree Press
Merrion Building
Lower Merrion Street
Dublin 2, Ireland
http://www.oaktreepress.com

© 2000 Samuel A. Malone

A catalogue record of this book is
available from the British Library.

ISBN 1 86076 170 4

Printed in the Republic of Ireland
by Colour Books Ltd.

Contents

Acknowledgements

Tony Buzan is the creator of Mind Maps®. The term "Mind Maps®" is the registered trademark of Tony Buzan.

The inventor of the SQ3R system is Professor R.P. Robinson.

Although most of the mnemonics used in the text are my own invention, some have been acquired over the years in my role as a trainer and educationalist. If made known, I will gladly acknowledge the source of these in future editions.

Some of the learning models used in this book appeared originally in my book *Success Skills for Managers*, published by Oak Tree Press in 1999.

The PLAN system of memory and the DEEP AIR mnemonic for laws of learning first appeared in my book *Mind Skills for Managers*, published by Gower in 1997.

The RTQPARM approach to answering examination questions, and the mnemonic FRAMEWORK for the advantages of learning maps, first appeared in my book *Learning to Learn*, published by CIMA in 1996.

Every attempt has been made to trace and acknowledge copyright material. The author and publisher will be happy to acknowledge copyright in future editions.

I am grateful to David Givens, Brian Langan and the team at Oak Tree Press for their thoroughness and efficiency in bringing this book to press.

Preface

Lifelong learning skills are essential for managers to survive in the job market. Whether you are an aspiring or an experienced manager, this book will help you to exploit the learning opportunities of the future. This book will show you the best way to learn on the job and the best way to study and prepare for exams at third level or beyond, whether you are coming back to education or simply pursuing lifelong learning, and whether your learning goal is job-related or to fulfil your personal development needs. All the management gurus agree that learning to learn is the most vital skill for success in a management career in the modern world. The ability of an organisation to learn and to go on learning is a key competitive advantage. This book will help managers to learn effectively on- or off-the-job.

Human beings are learning machines. We are continually learning until the day we die. Don't leave learning to chance. Follow the systematic approach in this book and become a better learner in all areas of your life. We now know more about the human brain and how people learn than ever before. Your objective should be to acquire this knowledge in order to advance your career.

This book is divided into 11 chapters. Each chapter is introduced with a series of questions. People learn more effectively if they seek answers to questions posed. Each chapter concludes with a summary and a learning map. The summaries and learning maps enable you to get a quick overview and review of the key ideas in the book. **Chapter 1** provides a brief overview of your brain. It includes the latest research on the learning potential of your brain. There is no computer currently available as complex or sophisticated as the human brain, and yet you get no instruction on how to use it. If you look after your brain, it will serve you well into ripe old age.

Chapter 2 is about key learning skills for managers and includes the learning cycle, learning styles and the four types of learning. The four stages of learning and the four learning styles of activist, reflector, theorist and pragmatist are discussed. The four types of learning — unlearning, new learning, incremental learning and transformational learning — are explored. Learning from experience at work is shown to be as important as any other type of learning. The chapter also discusses how we can learn more effectively if we are able to identify and eliminate the barriers to learning. Learning laws give us a simple and quick overview of how learning is facilitated. Some of the best ideas in learning are contained in the nine Cs of learning.

Chapter 3 is about improving your learning IQ. The seven intelligences are explored, as is emotional IQ. The importance of learning by objectives is highlighted. Identifying your learning needs, drawing up learning objectives, designing personal development plans and evaluating the effectiveness of your learning is covered. Some lessons are drawn from the lives of great scientific and historical figures who showed great ability, innovation and persistence in learning, often in the face of great hardship and adversity. One of the basic models of learning is the VAK model, which means that we mainly learn from visual, auditory and kinaesthetic or tactile experiences. Psychological and other factors in learning are also discussed.

Chapter 4 is about the learning organisation. In a changing world, learning is one of the key competitive factors and so organisations are keen to know how they can become learning organisations. New core beliefs and values are needed. The role of the manager in facilitating learning is explored. The triggers and inhibitors of a learning organisation are discussed. A useful learning model is analysed.

Chapter 5 is about learning opportunities and resources. Learning resources include biography work, learning sets, learning logs, networking and diagnostic instruments. The ASPIRE self-development model is a good template for planning your career.

The performance potential model shows how some managers get stuck in a rut. The career life cycle is explored, as is the phenomenon of managers plateauing. Benchmarking is a great way of learning from the best practices of others. Learning from change and learning to learn are the key survival skills for the future.

Chapter 6 is all about accelerated learning. It provides practical skills for improving your everyday ability to learn faster and smarter. Learning maps, effective reading, memory and concentration skills are explored. These are the types of skills that will make you a more effective learner.

Chapter 7 is all about making the best use of your time for work and for study. Your learning experiences should be planned. A time management model is discussed. The PASS model for effective study is highlighted. A knowledge of biorhythms may help you plan study at times when you are most alert. A time contract should be drawn up to show your commitment to effective time management.

Chapter 8 is all about effective writing. At work, writing skills are essential for preparing memos or reports. Many managers are now pursuing third-level or postgraduate qualifications and writing skills are needed to do assignments and dissertations and of course when sitting examinations. A research model for a thesis is suggested and a systematic approach to report writing is provided. The chapter includes a useful checklist for writing a better thesis.

Chapter 9 is all about examination technique. Many managers now undertake third-level and postgraduate qualifications to enhance their promotional prospects or to acquire greater expertise in their current jobs. This chapter is designed with these people in mind. It is probably many years since you formally studied and your exam skills have become rusty. Now is the time to brush up. Multiple-choice questions are a feature of many modern exams. A suggested approach to tackling this type of exam is suggested. A systematic approach to solving case studies in exams, which is a feature of management education, is included.

Chapter 10 is all about on-the-job learning, which is the most important source of learning for managers. LAYGO, or learning as you go techniques, such as self-directed learning, self-reflection, learning from mistakes, continuous improvement, career development, action learning and just-in-time learning are included. A whole range of on-the-job learning experiences are discussed, including project work, meetings, work shadowing, job enrichment, coaching and mentoring. The CRAMP on-the-job learning model and the KASH model are overviewed. The competencies needed to be successful in a management job are highlighted.

Chapter 11 is all about off-the-job learning. Off-the-job learning may include academic courses, courses run by training organisations and involvement in outside bodies. There are a wide range of off-the-job learning approaches, including outdoor experiential learning, business games, T-groups, role play, case studies, secondment, sabbaticals, demonstrations, in-tray exercises and simulations. The important role of assessment centres and corporate learning centres are overviewed.

List of Figures

1

The Brain — Your Biocomputer

*"Men ought to know that from the brain, and from the
brain only, arise our pleasures, joys, laughter, as well as
our sorrows, pains, griefs and tears. Through it, in
particular, we think, see, hear, and distinguish
the ugly from the beautiful, the bad from the good,
the pleasant from the unpleasant." — Hippocrates*

♦ *How is the brain organised?*

♦ *How can I integrate both sides of the brain?*

♦ *What are brain waves?*

♦ *What is the difference between the male and female brain?*

♦ *What is the LION model for brain maintenance?*

♦ *Does the brain age?*

♦ *What is Artificial Intelligence?*

Historical Perspective

The brain is the final frontier awaiting discovery. We know more
about outer space than about inner space. Nevertheless, in the last
20 years much progress has been made by the scientific community
in finding out how our brain works and how we should look after it
to keep it at peak performance during our lifetime. In fact, scientists have learned more about the brain in the last five years than
in the previous 100. It remains a source of amazement and mystery

and a focus of much research. The brain is the centre of learning. Most people don't appreciate the marvellous biocomputer they carry around in their head. It has outstanding information-processing capacity and we need to know what action we should take to maintain its learning efficiency.

The analogy between the brain and a computer does not do the brain sufficient justice. The power of the biggest computer is insignificant when compared with the capacity of the human brain. Like a computer, brain cells produce electrical signals and send them from cell to cell along pathways called circuits. Similar to a computer, these circuits receive, process, store, and retrieve information. Unlike a computer, however, the brain creates its electrical signals by chemical means. The proper functioning of the brain depends on the interaction of many complicated chemicals produced by brain cells.

The brain's capacity for language, creativity, artistic genius and common sense is unlikely to be rivalled by any computer now or in the future. This connected mass of grey matter, white matter, neurons, electrical impulses and chemical transmitters results in our thoughts, emotions and actions. Despite its complexity and what we know about it today, we are taught very little about how it functions. When you buy a computer, you get detailed instructional manuals on how to use it. However, our educational system provides us with little or no information on how to use our brain.

The Egyptians and the Greeks thought the mind was housed in the heart. In the fifth century BC, Hippocrates got it right, but scholars still maintained that thinking took place in the soul. It was not until the Renaissance that philosopher René Descartes concluded that thinking takes place in the brain. Today, electronic imaging technology has confirmed that he was right. These devices can now actually photograph the thinking processes of the brain in action. The sides of the brain engaged by different mental activities can readily be seen and studied.

Organisation of the Brain

Your brain can be divided into three interconnected constituent brains. These are called the neocortex, the reptilian and the mammalian brain. Together they make up the triune brain. These show that the human brain has evolved over millions of years. The neocortex or cerebrum, with its crinkly folds and fissures, is the most recent addition. It is divided into two hemispheres, which in turn are further divided into lobes. The neocortex covers the top of the brain forming a wrinkled layer of grey matter. It takes up most of the space in the skull. Its size and sophisticated structure separates man from the other primates and animals. In here resides your ability to think, plan, analyse, solve problems, have insights and make judgements.

The neocortex is the most recently evolved part of the cerebral cortex. The neocortex has its full complement of nerve cells at birth. Even if an individual lives to a ripe old age, no new nerve cells are formed in this part of the brain. Yet the most rapid growth of the neocortex occurs in the first ten years of life.

Scientists have identified four lobes of the neocortex and we now know a little about their functions. The frontal lobes are involved in the planning and control of movement. Damage to the frontal lobes can cause serious personality and behaviour changes. You may experience violent mood swings and find it difficult to plan and make decisions. The occipital lobes process visual information and then send it on to the parietal and temporal lobes. Damage to the occipital lobes may result in problems with your vision. The parietal lobes process information from the skin, muscles and joints, while the temporal lobe processes information from the ears. Damage to the parietal lobes may affect your spatial perception and you may have problems with reading. Also, you may be unable to identify simple everyday objects. Damage to the temporal lobes may cause problems with your hearing.

The mammalian brain marks an earlier stage of our evolution. In here resides the limbic system and the hippocampus. The limbic system is the seat of our feelings and emotions like love, affection, hate, sorrow, anxiety and joy. Our pleasure centre is located here. It also controls our metabolism for important functions such as hormones, sleep, thirst, hunger, heart rate, body temperature and the immune system.

The hippocampus has an important role in memory and filters information through to the neocortex for long-term memory storage. The hippocampus is especially important for processing and remembering spatial and contextual information. Spatial information would include the route to the airport and contextual information includes where you left your car when visiting the supermarket.

The reptilian brain marks the earliest stage of our evolution and, as you can guess, we share this with the reptiles. Scientists believe this part of the brain developed more than 500 million years ago. The reptilian brain has no language facility but looks after most of your physical wellbeing. The sensory motor functions are controlled from here, as are your primitive instincts such as the fight or flight response, the territorial instinct and the survival instinct.

Brain Hemispheres

It is now well established that your brain is made up of two halves or hemispheres. The left hemisphere controls the right-hand side of the body while the right hemisphere controls the left-hand side of the body. Similarly, the visual field is split down the middle and crossed. The left visual field travels to the right side of the brain. The right visual field travels to the left side of the brain.

Damage in one side of the brain may result in paralysis of the opposite side of the body. Much of what is known about brain function has been found by studying people with brain damage or split brain patients after lobotomy operations. The left brain is our rational brain. It deals with language, logic and mathematical relationships. It processes written and spoken information. Accounting, computer programming and operational research are left-brain professions. Left and right brain functions are illustrated in the following diagram:

Newton, the inventor of calculus and the scientific method, had a highly developed rational brain. Galileo, with a supreme logical mind, devised experiments, made careful observations and expressed his findings in mathematical terms. Western civilisation puts a great emphasis on the rational (left) side of the brain. For example, Frederick Taylor, the "Father of Scientific Management", believed that there was one best way for doing anything. These days, we believe in continuous improvement. Writing, reading and arithmetic, all left brain skills, are the core disciplines of our primary educational system.

The right brain is our creative brain. It deals with rhyme, rhythm, music and art. It interprets information visually, creatively and emotionally. Systems analysts, management consultants and strategic planners would need right brain skills. There is evidence that right-brain damage results in some loss of appreciation of humour, metaphor, face recognition and the ability to follow a story-line. Left-brain damage may affect our language abilities, such as speech and writing. Eastern civilisation puts an emphasis on right brain skills such as intuition, paradox, ambiguity and uncertainty.

The Interconnected Brain

It would be wrong to think that your two hemispheres are independent of one another. They are interconnected by the corpus callosum, the communication link between the two. The functions of the two hemispheres are not as specialised as previously thought. Although writing is considered a left-brain skill, it is now known to require the co-operation of both hemispheres. The verbal aspect of writing is logical, but the actual process of writing uses motor and visual skills.

Parts of the brain seem to specialise in specific skills. For example, Broca's area is devoted to speech, while Wernicke's area is devoted to comprehension of the spoken and written word. In fact, Wernicke advanced the first evidence for the idea of distributed processing, which is the modern view of mental functions. Wernicke proposed that only the most primary mental functions, those concerned with simple perceptual and motor activities, are localised to a single area of the brain. More complex intellectual functions result from interconnections among several functional sites. Broca's and Wernicke's areas are in different parts of the left hemisphere. Damage to these areas of the brain may adversely affect language skills, although other faculties such as intelligence and memory may remain intact. Long-term memory and intelligence are thought to be spread over the entire cerebral hemisphere.

The original Renaissance man and whole brain thinker was Leonardo Da Vinci, who had both scientific and artistic talents. Modern life encourages specialisation, but we still come across an all-round genius like the American architect Buckminster Fuller. There is now a realisation of the importance of developing both sides of your brain, as evidenced in the more holistic approach taken in learning and medicine.

Integrating Both Sides of the Brain

If you understand how each side of your brain works, you can adopt appropriate strategies to help you integrate both sides of your brain and maximise your learning effectiveness. The mnemonic INHALED will help you to remember some of the strategies you can undertake to integrate both sides of the brain:

- **Imagination or visualisation**. Visualisation is a right-brain function. Psychologists have found that individuals who visualise a finished product or end result are more successful in achieving their goals or solving problems. Therefore, in a learning situation, you should try to visualise and experience the outcome as vividly as possible. The ability to change the unconscious through affirmations and visualisation is an important aspect of accelerated learning. In addition, when reading you should translate the words into pictures to engage both sides of the brain for better learning and recall.

- **Notes of music**. Music and rhythm are right-brain functions. Classical music, and baroque music in particular, has been found to facilitate learning. Jingles, rhythms and rhymes, as advertising practitioners are well aware, facilitate the learning and retention of advertising messages. The idea that prolonged listening to the works of great classical composers can enhance brain development in infants has been called the "Mozart Effect". It is based on the fact that a child's ability to reason, listen and learn develops rapidly until the age of six and then levels off. Monks learn the psalms by chanting the words. Children learn the alphabet as a rhyme. The Bulgarian psychologist Georgi Lozanov found that baroque music puts learners into a state of alert relaxation. In this state, learners enhance their ability to learn and memorise.

- **Humour**. Humour draws on left-brain, rational processes and on right-brain creative processes. The inclusion of humorous material in learning situations will help to integrate both sides of the brain. When you laugh, your brain secretes endorphin, a natural hormone that has a painkilling and tranquillising effect on the body. The result is a feeling of wellbeing and a state of relaxation, which facilitates learning.

- **Analogy**. The right brain likes links, associations, metaphors and analogies. Linking and associating ideas from different disciplines will stimulate right-brain processing. Jesus used parables to explain complex religious themes. Good speakers and trainers use metaphors and stories to engage the imagination of their audience.

- **Learning maps**. Learning maps (see page 155) use both sides of the brain. The words and logic of learning maps call on left-brain processing. Their radiant, non-linear format, with diagrams, pictures, symbols and colour, call on right-brain skills. So by drawing learning maps you integrate both sides of the brain and thus maximise your capacity to learn.

- **Emotionalise**. The more emotions are involved, the more information will be registered in the right brain. Emotions drive attention, which in turn drives learning, memory, problem-solving and concentration. Emotions help to focus and intensify or otherwise our level of concentration. We are more likely to remember situations in which our emotions are heightened, such as waiting for an important decision to be made or an im-

portant letter to arrive, or our wedding day. Information that is
processed by both the right and left sides of the brain is more
likely to be remembered. Action learning, which employs visual,
auditory and tactile senses, facilitates integrated learning.

- **Diagrams**. As a learner, you should always represent ideas
  and concepts in the form of diagrams. Diagrams and flow charts
  simplify and clarify problems, facilitate overview and encourage
  both left-brain and right-brain processing.

The Capacity of the Brain

The capacity of the brain is enormous. Scientists estimate that we
have between 10 billion and 100 billion brain cells. Each brain cell
is connected to between 10,000 and 50,000 other brain cells. These
brain cells are connected by dendrites, which grow as we get older
and acquire more experience. Impulses are received by the brain
cell and passed as a pulse of electric charge. The axon ends at the
synapse (junction with other brain cells) and releases a chemical
neurotransmitter, which jumps across to the next cell. Nerve impulses travel quickly and may reach speeds of 525 feet per second.

Learning occurs through a change in the strength of certain synaptic connections. A frequently used synapse becomes stronger,
whereas an infrequently used one may grow weaker over time. Scientists have found that in Wernicke's area, which deals with word
understanding, the nerve cells have more dendrites in third-level
educated people than in people with only second-level education.

The more connections you have, the better your brain works.
This probably, in the healthy brain, more than compensates for any
loss of brain cells thought to occur during a lifetime. So you can be
smarter at 50 than you were at 20. Some scientists estimate that
above 40 to 50 years of age, we lose about 2 per cent of our brain
cells every decade. Others have found that some areas of the brain
do not lose nerve cells at all with ageing. Apparently, the loss of
cells varies from region to region.

There is some evidence that the decrease in brain weight and the
extent of nerve cell loss in healthy old people is relatively slight. A
few of the myths about the deterioration of functioning during

ageing are slowly being replaced as scientific knowledge offers some contrary evidence. However, we have more brain cells than we'll ever need in a lifetime and the loss over a lifetime is relatively minuscule.

It is amazing that an organ weighing only 3.1 lbs and accounting for only 2 per cent of body weight has so much capacity. Information theorist John von Neumann once estimated that the memories stored during the average human lifespan would amount to 2.8×10^{20} or 280,000,000,000,000,000,000 bits, assuming nothing is forgotten.

The brain is a high consumer of energy and burns up to 25 per cent of the calories we consume, enough to light a 15 to 25 watt bulb. It also produces its own painkillers. The human brain uses 20 per cent of the oxygen used by the entire body when at rest.

Our cerebral cortex is 3mm thick and covers an area of 2,360 sq. cm or 354 sq. in. Two-thirds of our brain mass consists of the two hemispheres, which are wrapped around all the other parts. Research has found that the left hemisphere is anatomically larger than the right. It is also more active than the right in most adults.

Watching the Brain at Work

Positron emission tomography (PET) and functional magnetic resonance imaging (fMRI) are safe new technologies similar to X-rays that enable scientists to watch the healthy, living, active brain at work. PET shows the parts of the brain that are using the most glucose, a form of sugar. fMRI shows the parts of the brain using high oxygen levels, which indicate increased brain activity. The output is shown on computer screens as colour-coded maps.

The way we learn, the way our memory works and what parts of the brain are engaged in various mental and physical activities can all be seen and studied on screen. For example, PET scan studies suggest that the left side of the prefrontal cortex is involved in the acquisition of new information, while the right specialises in later recall. PET scan studies have also shown that mental rehearsal shows the same pattern on screen as the actual activity. It seems that as far as the brain is concerned, imagining something in your head is not very much different than actually doing it.

Sometimes other parts of the brain can be trained to take over the functions of damaged parts. Damage through stroke to Wernicke's area causes difficulty in understanding language. However, some people with this condition have been helped to speak again through intensive speech therapy. PET scans showed that other parts of the brain were rewired during the speech therapy to compensate for the damaged Wernicke's area.

Brain Waves

A knowledge of how brain waves function may help us enhance our learning abilities. Brain waves can be recorded and studied on an electroencephalogram (EEG). There are four types of brain waves:

1. **Beta waves** are the most common and they happen when we are alert during normal mental activities. They occur at the highest frequency of between 13 and 30 cycles per second. If you feel yourself blocked by a problem, you are almost certainly in a beta mode.

2. **Alpha waves** occur when we are relaxed and experiencing pleasant feelings. A lack of alpha waves suggests anxiety and stress. People learn faster and remember more when physically relaxed. Ornstein found that when a person was doing maths, the EEG showed that the left hemisphere was active and in beta mode. However, the EEG also showed an increase in alpha mode in the right hemisphere. Thus, alpha mode allows for better integration of the two hemispheres of the brain. In general, the brain waves of clever people are more co-ordinated and coherent. This facilitates high levels of mental functioning.

3. **Theta waves** occur during moments of reverie, often just before we are about to fall asleep or before we actually wake up. These are at a low frequency of 4–7 cycles per second. They may also occur during daydreaming. People often get their most creative and inspiring ideas during theta waves. Theta waves occur naturally during periods of meditation.

4. **Delta waves** occur during sleep. It is not possible to learn during sleep. However, there is some evidence to suggest that

learning up to the time we go asleep can be very effective. It seems that sleep consolidates learning and the less activity and interference between the learning task and sleep the better.

Male versus Female Brain

Although male and female brains are very similar, some differences have been discovered. The male brain is about 10 per cent bigger than the female brain. However, relative brain size does not make a difference. Intelligence is mostly determined by the number of connections between brain cells, rather than size. Jonathan Swift's brain weighed 4.4 pounds. However, Albert Einstein had a normal-sized brain while Anatole France, who won the Nobel Prize for literature, had a brain that weighed only 2.2 pounds. Scientists believe it was the richness of connections in Einstein's brain and the use he made of it that accounts for much of his genius. Concentrated thinking shapes the brain with the strengthening of existing connections and the laying down of new connections. Thinking is good for your brain.

Psychological testing consistently shows that the average man performs better than the average woman on spatial tasks, such as visualising objects in three dimensions. Women, on the other hand, do better than men on tests involving writing, reading and vocabulary. But this average difference in ability is small. Many men are better at language than the average for women, and many women have better spatial skills than the average for men.

The male has a thicker right hemisphere, which may account for his reported edge in visual and spatial tasks such as reading a map. On the other hand, the female brain has a thicker left hemisphere, which may account for her edge in fluency and language skills. Females are better at fine motor control, which would suggest that they would make superior surgeons.

Imaging technology studies of men and women reading or thinking about words show differences. These studies have found that men generally use only their left cerebral hemisphere for processing language, but women use both hemispheres.

The male has less brain cells than the female and loses brain cells three times faster. In line with mortality statistics, the female brain survives eight years longer than the male brain. The female brain has a larger corpus callosum, which may suggest that the female brain is more integrated and holistic. This may account for "feminine intuition" and make women more emotionally intelligent.

Men's brains are more specialised and are more vulnerable to dyslexia and hyperactivity. There are more left-handed men than women, and boys with learning disabilities far outnumber girls. Some scientists believe when the foetus produces excess testosterone, it stunts the growth of the left hemisphere, causing left-handedness and learning disorders. Men tend to have more difficulty recovering from strokes or brain injuries. The more specialised male brain may account for their supposed superiority in maths, engineering and science.

The LION Model

LION is a mnemonic which stands for Love, Information, Oxygen and Nutrition. The brain cannot survive without these four vital ingredients. Without stimulation, nurturing, recognition and care, the brain will deteriorate. Use the LION model to maximise care and maintenance of your brain. The LION model is illustrated in the following diagram:

LION MODEL

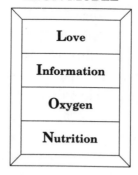

| Love |
| Information |
| Oxygen |
| Nutrition |

Love

Your brain needs love, affection, appreciation and positive thinking if it is to thrive. Even premature babies need love and affection. Babies kept in incubators with a "no touch" sign failed to thrive. Researchers found that premature babies who were held and had their backs stroked thrived. Stress hormones declined and the babies doubled their growth rate. Premature babies are now routinely held and stroked and they develop at a more normal rate.

Satisfying emotional needs is essential at any age. Research shows that ageing rats that were given some tender loving care were able to increase their life span in comparison to rats that did not get the same attention. This suggests that the limbic system and the cortex need to work in harmony for the wellbeing of the whole person. It is now generally accepted that the emotions play an important part in learning. This is recognised in the contribution of emotional intelligence to overall wellbeing. An enriched emotional environment enhances brain development.

Information

The plasticity of your brain is now accepted. This means that your brain can rewire itself in response to environmental stimuli and learning. Individual brains can differ significantly, depending on a person's background and experience. The fingers activate the same general area of the sensory cortex in everyone's brain. But this area is larger in people who use their fingers particularly often. Examples include musicians who play stringed instruments, or blind people who read Braille.

Modern imaging techniques can show how learning stimulates your brain. PET scans show that the brains of people skilled in a particular area consume less energy than those just starting to learn it. The experienced brains have generated new synaptic connections, which improves their performance. Feed the brain with information and the connections between the brain cells, called dendrites, increase.

Starve your brain of information and the dendrites wither and die off. In sensory deprivation experiments, where people are kept in complete isolation, skills built up over a lifetime can quickly deteriorate. Your brain depends on stimulation from the environment. Passive observation is not enough; one must interact with the environment. It is the interaction of the environment with heredity which has changed the dimensions of the human brain over millions of years. It seems experience changes the dendritic map of the brain throughout your life. Lifelong learning feeds it. Failure to ex-

ercise your mind kills it. Always asking questions and seeking answers provides continuous stimulation to your brain cells. It's a
question of using your brain or losing it.

Education is food for the brain. The cerebral cortex grows rapidly
in the first ten years of a child's life. By providing a stimulating environment during this period, the growth of dendritic connections
will be facilitated. This merely supports what educationalists have
long known: that providing a wide variety of experiences to the
growing child enhances intellectual development. So mental exercise does far more than just increase your knowledge. It increases
the size of your brain and the number of dendritic connections between your brain cells. On the other hand, old people put in a retirement home without adequate mental stimulation become senile
and dependent. However, the opposite happens if they are challenged by learning experiences and given responsibility and control
over their own lives.

Oxygen

Your brain needs oxygen to survive. Your brain can go without oxygen for only three to five minutes before serious damage results.
Starved of oxygen, your brain will die. Reduced oxygen to your
brain will impair mental processing and memory storage and retrieval. Aerobic exercise increases blood-flow to your brain and
burns off harmful stress hormones. Smoking reduces the oxygen
flow to your brain and so is bad for your brain as well as for your
lungs and general health. Lack of exercise also reduces oxygen flow
to your brain.

Nutrition

It is now known that your brain needs a rich nutritional diet. An
adequate supply of nutrients and vitamins is needed for peak body
and brain performance. This is nothing new. It was Plato who said
in 400 BC that a healthy body promotes a healthy brain and a
healthy brain, a healthy body. A balanced diet and exercise is essential for a healthy brain and body. A healthy diet stabilises blood
sugar levels, which is the only source of fuel for your brain. You

may be able to extend the life of your brain by up to 50 per cent by cutting down on your food intake. Rats fed on a restricted calorie diet lived 50 per cent longer. So eating less is probably very good for both your body and brain.

Low blood sugar causes poor concentration and prevents memories from being laid down. Korsakoff's syndrome, often caused by alcoholism and an associated lack of thiamine or vitamin B1, can cause amnesia and permanent loss of memory. Some vitamins, such as thiamine, folic acid, and B12, are essential for the proper working of memory. They are found in bread and cereals, vegetables and fruits. Some research suggests that vitamins C and E have a role in keeping the memory sharp. Primrose oil also apparently can help to keep at bay the kind of memory loss associated with advancing age. Water helps maintain memory, especially in older people. Dehydration can generate confusion and other thought problems.

Stress and the Brain

The hippocampus plays a vital role in the laying down of our memories. Magnetic resonance imaging has shown decreases in volume in the hippocampus of people who have suffered severe stress or trauma. However, imaging also shows that this neuronal damage and shrinkage of the hippocampus can be reversed, provided the stress does not go on too long.

Stress produces a chemical in the brain called cortisol, which actively kills brain cells. Moderate amounts of cortisol are not harmful. However, chronic stress over a long period can produce large amounts of cortisol, which kills and injures billions of brain cells. Research shows that chronic stress has an adverse effect on your ability to remember. Just like the body, your brain needs rest and relaxation. While sleeping, your brain disconnects from the senses and revises and stores memories. Lack of sleep impairs your ability to concentrate and lay down new memories. Baroque music with a beat of 60 beats a minute is especially beneficial for relaxing your brain. Also, meditation quietens and rests your brain.

Age and the Brain

A long-standing myth is that intelligence peaks in adolescence and then deteriorates. In fact, your brain does not reach its maximum weight until you are about 30 years of age. Better news still is that the integration of the right side with the left side is not fully developed until you are 40 years of age. Because connections between brain cells increase as you age, you are probably smarter at 50 than you were at 20. Although there is some evidence that the brain does deteriorate after 60, this deterioration is very gradual and, for all practical purposes in the healthy brain, is minuscule.

Ageism has arisen in the Western world as life expectancy has increased and the actual retirement age for many people is getting lower and lower. People over the young age of 35 are often discriminated against when applying for jobs. Some may only be taken on in less-well-paid jobs or on a part-time basis. Many companies are reluctant to invest in the training of older employees. They assume that they are less flexible and slow to adapt to new ideas.

Old Brains are the Best

But what is the reality? We know that wisdom grows with experience and age. Politicians, judges, scientists, entertainers, writers, chief executives and medical specialists are all considered very young at 50 and are often considered only in their prime when well into their 60s and 70s. In politics, Nelson Mandela, De Gaulle and Churchill are only some of the politicians that made it late in life. De Gaulle was in politics until he was 79. Mandela, after spending 26 years in prison for his opposition to the apartheid policies of South Africa, was elected deputy president of the African National Congress at the age of 72.

In the artistic field, Picasso produced some of his best work late in life. Goethe finished writing *Faust* at 82 years of age. George Bernard Shaw, the famous Irish writer, was still very active in his 70s. Adam Smith remains a towering figure in the history of economic thought. He was 53 years old when *The Wealth of Nations* was published, which is the age that many people now take early retirement. Skinner, the originator of programmed learning, produced some of his best work late in life.

In the entertainment business, Frank Sinatra, Marlene Dietrich and Joe Locke all performed successfully until very late in life. In education, it is not uncommon for people in their 50s, 60s and 70s to successfully complete third-level and postgraduate qualifications. Except in circumstances of poor health, evidence suggests there is little or no decline in energy and intellectual levels with age.

Another myth is that sexual activity begins an irreversible decline in the middle years. In fact, it has been established that sexual activity continues into the very late years of life. Ageism has been manufactured by the fashion and television industry for commercial reasons. It overemphasises youth and glamour and this attitude has been followed blindly by the leaders of industry and commerce.

Some companies are now beginning to question the wisdom of early retirement. They are now realising that when experienced people leave a company, there is a huge loss of intellectual capital, which is a real financial loss despite the fact that it is not quantified on the Balance Sheet. The collective culture, wisdom, memory and experience of the company are being eroded. In many cases, the early retired come back as consultants to the company that retired them in the first place! In other instances, management consultants are hired from outside to fill the gap. Many firms that have let people go under early retirement schemes have found too late that they have lost their most loyal, experienced and skilled people. These retirees in turn have often set up successful businesses in competition with their previous employers.

Mimicking Brain Power

Artificial intelligence (AI) is the study of how to make computers do things that human brains can do. Robotic systems and expert systems have been modelled on the brain. The computer has sometimes been used as a model to understand some of the complexities of the brain. In practice, scientists have found it very difficult to mimic human creativity, its ability to learn from experience, the subtlety of human movements, the richness of human memory and the uniqueness of common sense. However, considerable progress has been made and will continue to be made in the future. Artificial intelligence is an enhancement and extension to human brainpower rather than a replacement.

Expert systems are used extensively in all area of business. Expert systems can make medical diagnoses as good as any doctor. Even the world chess champion Gary Kasparov was beaten by a computer in 1997. Computers are now used to predict the weather and share prices. AI-generated music is now commonplace. AI robots are used by the army for bomb disposal and have been used in space exploration. In industry, AI robots can do boring, dirty, or dangerous jobs, sometimes in places that humans cannot reach.

Virtual reality is a computer program, coupled with other tools and devices, that enable a person to perform tasks "virtually" with all the experiences of a real situation. For example, trainee pilots in a flight simulator can feel the effects of flying when in fact they are still stationery on the ground. Virtual reality can help architects understand what rooms look like in the inside of a house. Interior designers can visit each room in a house and move around, manipulate objects, and interact with other visitors inside the building. To experience virtual reality, a person may need to wear powerful dataglasses, as well as a special helmet, computerised clothing, datagloves, and lightwave body sensors.

Summary

The brain can be divided into three parts. The neocortex is what makes us essentially human and gives us our power to plan, think, analyse and solve problems. The mammalian brain plays an important role in memory, feelings and metabolism, such as body temperature and hormones. The reptilian brain is where our primitive instincts, such as the survival instinct, are located. All parts of the brain are highly integrated and co-operate with each other.

The neocortex is divided into two hemispheres. The left hemisphere is mainly concerned with logic and language. The right hemisphere is mainly concerned with art and music. People have the capacity for both logic and artistic abilities.

A model for integrating both sides of your brain, INHALED, was discussed. This stands for:

- **I**magination or visualisation
- **N**otes of music
- **H**umour
- **A**nalogy
- **L**earning maps
- **E**motionalise
- **D**iagrams.

A knowledge of how brain waves operate may help us to learn faster and remember more.

Scientists have found some physical differences between the male and female brains, which may help account for our unique strengths and talents.

The model LION was used as a device for maximising care and maintenance of the brain. This stands for:

- **L**ove
- **I**nformation
- **O**xygen
- **N**utrition.

Artificial intelligence has been successfully applied to expert systems, robotics and automated manufacturing systems. It is unlikely that the common sense and creativity of humans can ever be modelled. Artificial intelligence is an extension to human brainpower, rather than a replacement.

Modern culture tends to stereotype the old. Organisations have gone along with this conventional wisdom and hence older employees are the first to go during times of restructuring and downsizing. There is now evidence to suggest that in general older people are smarter than younger people. As you age, provided you keep mentally active, the number of connections between your brain cells actually increases. This more than compensates for any loss of brain cells. You are probably smarter at 50 than you are at 20. The biographies of many famous people who peaked in their later years would support this viewpoint.

CHAPTER 1 LEARNING MAP

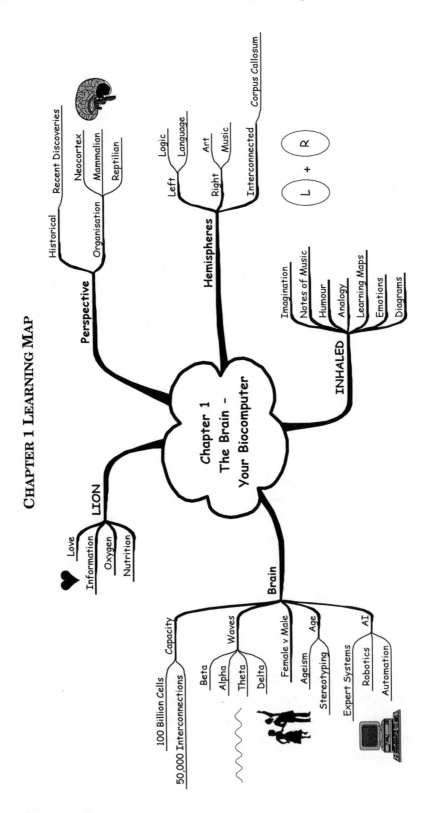

2

Effective Learning for Managers

"What one knows is, in youth, of little moment; they know enough who know how to learn." — Henry Adams

---

♦ *How do adults learn?*

♦ *What is the learning cycle?*

♦ *What are learning styles?*

♦ *What are the stages of learning?*

♦ *What is the UNIT model of learning?*

♦ *What are the laws of learning?*

♦ *What are the 9Cs of learning?*

♦ *How can I learn from experience?*

Introduction

Much of the information on learning is contained in academic texts that generally are inaccessible and unintelligible to the average busy manager. This chapter sets out to take you on a journey of the best concepts and ideas currently available to managers. We know more about the learning process than ever before. Many of these ideas if implemented would make you a much more effective and thoughtful learner, both on and off the job. Treat the content of the chapter like a menu. Relish the bits that suit your purpose and discard those you find less useful.

Characteristics of Adult Learners

You, as a manager, are different from children or young students because of your accumulated experience and responsibilities. The following are some points about the typical adult learner that you should keep in mind about yourself as a learner:

- You see yourself as independent and self-directed. You like to have control over and be responsible for your own learning.

- You have a lot of experience which you like to share with others.

- You are goal-oriented and relevancy-centred. You are motivated by the prospect of achieving goals and you like to know why you are learning something.

- You are practical and like to solve problems. You like to learn things that will be useful in your career or to your self-development.

- You are sometimes intimated by formal learning situations and you do not like to lose face.

- Because of your life responsibilities, you have preoccupations other than learning.

- You have set habits, find it hard to change, but you can change.

- In a formal learning situation, you prefer instructors to adopt a facilitator style rather than a lecturing style. Learning strategies such as case studies, role-playing, discussion, simulations and self-evaluations are most useful. As Ivan Illich said: "Most learning is not the result of instruction. It is rather the result of unhampered participation in a meaningful setting."

What is Learning?

Mumford (1997) discusses how Reg Revan formulated a simple model of learning: $L = P + Q$. This means learning is equal to programmed knowledge plus questions. During their training, specialists acquire a whole codified system of knowledge related to their speciality. "P" can be thought of as techniques that can be learned to solve routine problems. On the other hand, "Q" activities deal with unprogrammed problems calling for creativity, judgement, intuition and insight. These are the types of abilities that are needed by successful managers and are developed through on-the-job experience rather than formal training.

Management is all about dealing with unprogrammed problems. There are no off-the-shelf solutions to these types of problems. Hence the risk involved in management decision-making. General managers need to be able to ask the right incisive questions to maximise specialist input and to manage effectively. Managers need to maintain an enquiring mind so that they will not be taken in by their functional experts. Otherwise managers can be blinded by science and confused by jargon!

Learning Cycle

David Kolb is the creator of the learning cycle. The learning styles of activist, reflector, theorist and pragmatist are linked to the learning cycle and we will explore these styles in the next section. The learning cycle highlights the importance of reflection and continuous improvement and learning. It is a simple idea, and simple ideas are the best. Newton said that simple laws explain complicated things. The mnemonic DRUD will help you remember the steps involved:

- **Do something**
- **Reflect on it**
- **Understand it (conclude)**
- **Do it differently**

The Learning Cycle is illustrated in the following diagram:

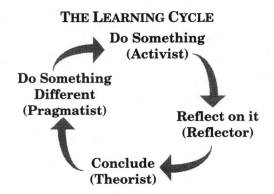

THE LEARNING CYCLE

Do Something (Activist)

Do Something Different (Pragmatist)

Reflect on it (Reflector)

Conclude (Theorist)

Do something (Activist)

In the real world of business, you learn by actually doing things, by identifying and exploiting opportunities. On-the-job learning is possibly the best type of learning. It brings all the senses, visual, auditory and tactile, to bear on the learning activity. On-the-job learning includes job enrichment, job enlargement and job rotation. It also includes mentoring, demonstrations, secondments, project work and overseas assignments (see Chapter 10). In formal training programmes, trainers try to mimic the real world by using models, simulations, role-play and case studies.

Reflect on it (Reflector)

At the end of each day, you should review your successes and failures and record them in a learning log or diary. Learning from your mistakes is the most effective form of learning. Aristotle believed that asking probing questions is the best way to learn. If you ask the right questions, you'll elicit the right answers. Directed curiosity about why certain things happen the way they do and cause-and-effect relationships will help you learn from the past. Apply questions like what, why, when, how, where and who to your experiences. How can you apply the lessons in the future to help you avoid repeating those mistakes made in the past and perform more effectively? One expert has called this process the "Santayana Review", quoting the famous philosopher George Santayana, who coined the phrase "Those who cannot remember the past are condemned to repeat it." Unfortunately, too many managers today are indifferent to the past and by failing to reflect on it, valuable lessons for the future are lost. Henry Ford is reputed to have said that thinking is the hardest work there is, which is probably the reason why so few do it.

Understand it (Theorist)

Make sense of your experiences. To get a greater insight into your experience, relate it to theoretical concepts and models. Practice, by nature, will always differ from theory. But the theory may help you understand your experiences better and thus help you do it better in the future. The trick is to take what is useful from the theory, apply it and discard the rest. All scientific knowledge has been acquired through carrying out experiments, carefully observing what went on, making any necessary adjustments and making sense of what happened. The latter is often followed by the formulation of scientific laws or mathematical formula such as Einstein's $E = MC^2$.

Do it differently (Pragmatist)

This is the final stage of the learning cycle. It means adapting your ideas if necessary and trying them out. You are exploring, discovering and finding out what works and what doesn't work. Certain actions elicit certain outcomes. It is only by changing our actions that we can hope to change the outcomes. If you keep on doing the same things you are going to get the same results. If something doesn't work, you need to try something else until you get the desired results. This feedback channels your energies and determination in a positive and constructive way. This will enable you to solve problems and make decisions. After this, the learning cycle starts again and continues its indefinite cycle. The learning cycle is thus a cycle of continuous feedback of learning and relearning.

The TRAP Model

People have different approaches to learning. Some people are inclined to be academic and are interested in theories and concepts. Others are more interested in the practical side of things. Adult learners in general like to get involved actively in their own development and to have a say in the running of their own jobs. They like to share their experiences and to be self-directing and problem-centred. Some learners are more left-brain dominant while others are more right-brain dominant. This means that some people are analytical and rational and prefer logical and sequential learning experiences. Others are creative and artistic and like plenty of interaction, visual/spatial experiences and role-play.

To develop our brainpower, we should engage in a variety of learning experiences. These should appeal to both the rational and artistic parts of the brain and to as many of our senses as possible. In particular, the visual (see), auditory (hear) and tactile (feel and touch) senses should be catered for. Educationalists now believe that you learn 10 per cent of what you read, 15 per cent of what you hear, but 80 per cent of what you experience.

Alan Mumford (1997) and Peter Honey have identified four types of learners. The four types can be identified by the mnemonic TRAP which stands for Theorist, Reflector, Activist and Pragmatist. These can be linked to the learning cycle as shown above.

- **Theorist**. Theorists tend to be detached, logical, analytical and rational. They are keen on basic assumptions, principles, models and systems thinking. They feel uncomfortable with ambiguous experiences, creative and lateral thinking. They like to organise different facts into coherent theories. They are good people to have around because of their objectivity. In a group situation, they may come up with interesting factually based alternatives and challenge the conventional wisdom. Theorists make good systems analysts.

- **Reflector**. Plato said, "The life which is unexamined is not worth living." Reflectors tend to think deeply about their experiences and consider them from different viewpoints. They like to consider the facts before they come to a conclusion. They tend to be cautious and have the philosophy of "look before you leap". At meetings, they seem to be quiet and detached but are good listeners. Part of their approach is to get as many different points of view as possible before making up their own minds. They like to think, reflect and plan. They do not like being rushed into making decisions. The Lord gave us two ends — one to sit on and the other to think with. Success depends on which one we use the most! Reflectors make good strategic planners.

- **Activist**. As the name suggests, activists enjoy getting things done. They are very much involved in the here and now. They enjoy learning new experiences irrespective of their practical application. They tend to be reactive rather than proactive. They thrive on crisis management. They enjoy brainstorming and lateral thinking. They love being involved in teamwork activities. They are gregarious, attention-seeking and like to be the life and soul of the party. They are more at home in operational management roles rather than strategic roles. They do not learn well from passive situations such as reading a book or listening to a lecture. Activists make good line managers.

- **Pragmatist**. As the name suggests, these people have a very practical bent. They can't wait to try out ideas, theories and techniques to see if they work in practice. Unlike activists, they like to see a link between what they've learned and how they plan to use it on the job. They are thus more proactive than reactive. They are the type of people who come back from a course bursting with ideas and very keen to apply them. They see problems as opportunities and threats as challenges. They know that there is a better way of doing things. They believe in the philosophy of continuous improvement. Pragmatists make good computer programmers.

Lessons from the Learning Styles

Most people have a mix of the four learning styles, with a preference for one or two. You can determine your learning styles by taking Honey and Mumford's learning styles questionnaire (1986), which takes about 20 minutes to complete and is very reliable for determining particular learning styles.

It is important to find out your learning preferences so that you can take corrective action on your weaker styles. Draw up an action plan specifying the actions you need to take to improve your weaker styles. Also, when selecting people for jobs, it might be a good idea to find out what particular learning style they prefer in order to place them into suitable roles. Some jobs place emphasis on certain learning styles rather than others. For example, general managers tend to be pragmatists and activists rather than reflectors and theorists. On the other hand, people in strategic planning and research and development would need to have strong reflector and theorist styles.

In a job where decisions have to be made quickly, it is unlikely that a reflector and theorist style would be suitable. On the other hand, in a strategic planning role, these styles would be essential for success. In a training situation, a course should be designed to appeal to the four learning styles or in certain cases to the preferential learning styles of participants, if that is known. It would be a good idea to get course participants to do a learning styles questionnaire before a course to ascertain their individual learning styles. Managers should do likewise before they coach their staff. They are thus in a position to adapt their coaching styles to the learning styles of their staff. Similarly, mentors can carry out their role more effectively if they are aware of their own learning styles and that of the mentoree. The following are based on Honey and Mumford's ideas on how to improve the various learning styles.

Improving Your Activist Style

- Do something new. Visit a part of your organisation that you haven't seen before. Talk to different functional specialists about their roles. Join a society which deals with matters outside your current experience. Take a different route to work. Change newspapers occasionally to get a different perspective on current affairs. Try out a new restaurant, preferably one from a different culture. Visit a museum at lunchtime. Don't always wait for other people to take the initiative; do things first yourself. When you are buying a new car, go for a different make this time rather than sticking to the same brand.

- In social situations and at conferences, introduce yourself first. At the supermarket checkout, exchange some friendly words with the checkout operator. Become more involved in your professional institute or trade union. Get involved in a political party and go door-to-door canvassing for your favourite parliamentary candidate.

- Change activities during the day. If you tend to be quiet and reserved, take the initiative at meetings by asking appropriate questions. If you tend to procrastinate, do it now.

- At professional institutes, charities, or local resident association meetings, put yourself forward for officer positions such as chairperson, secretary, public relations officer or education officer. Chair meetings, lead discussions and give presentations. These bodies are always looking for volunteers and such positions can be great learning, development and social opportunities.

- Get involved in business games, simulations, competitive teamwork tasks, projects, and role-play exercises (see Chapter 11). Be prepared to be thrown in at the deep end with a task you think is difficult or offers a challenge because of inadequate resources and adverse conditions.

Improving Your Reflector Style

- At meetings, become an observer of human behaviour. Study people's body language such as posture, voice, gestures, eye movements, expressions and reactions. Look for hidden agendas and see how disagreements are resolved. Spend some time thinking and reflecting on situations. In general, develop a philosophy of reflecting before you jump to conclusions. Look before you leap.

- Keep a learning log. Record your learning experiences at the end of each day and reflect on the lessons that can be learnt and applied in the future. See mistakes as learning opportunities rather than mini-disasters. Remember that your goal is continuous improvement and self-development. Managers should review their successes and failures, assess them systematically and draw lessons from them for application in the future.

- Do some in-depth research on a topic that interests you. Go to the library and ask the librarian for guidance. They are usually only too willing to help. Visit your local bookshop to see the latest publications on the subject. Invest in building up a good library of books, tapes, videos and CD-ROMS. Broaden your interest by learning a new subject each year.

- Practise looking at issues from three perspectives: your own, the other person's and a detached viewpoint. Write the points down and reflect on the issues involved. Try to draw an impartial conclusion based on the facts of the case. Do not ignore intuitive feelings about the issue, as these can sometimes be right. At work, produce carefully considered analyses and reports.

- Think before you act and listen and assimilate before you speak. Don't jump to conclusions but establish the facts first. Prepare yourself by research and planning.

Improving Your Theorist Style

- Read academic books on management and organisational development. Summarise each chapter in the form of a learning map. Keep these for reference and review occasionally. Study well-known theoretical models in management, such as the Product Life Cycle, the Growth Share Matrix, Maslow's Hierarchy of Needs, Blake and Mouton's Managerial Grid and Likert's Four Systems of Management (see Cole, 1995). These are snapshots of profound management philosophy.

- Look for flaws in other people's arguments. Become a devil's advocate. Study reports critically for illogical statements and to see what unsupported conclusions are arrived at and what inconsistencies arise. Study books critically to see what is factually based and what is mere opinion. Study systems and procedures in your workplace to spot unnecessary tasks, inefficient operations and duplication. Study forms to see if they can be improved by combination, rearrangement or elimination of unnecessary requirements.

- Develop a questioning approach to problems. Seek out the reasons for company policies and procedures by continually asking "Why?". You'll surprise yourself occasionally by discovering that there is no logical basis for some policies and procedures. Take part in a question-and-answer session. Teach high calibre people to ask searching questions.

Improving Your Pragmatist Style

- Develop expertise in a wide variety of practical management techniques. Examples would include critical path analysis, flow charts, decision trees, force field analysis, cause-and-effect diagrams, breakeven analysis, variance analysis, ratio analysis, Pareto analysis, discounted cash flow and cost/benefit analysis. Set yourself the objective of learning one technique per week. Become aware of the strengths and weaknesses of these techniques and determine the areas of work in which they can be applied.

- Collect information on self-development techniques such as problem-solving, creative thinking, assertiveness, presentation skills, memory skills, speed reading, transactional analysis, neuro-linguistic programming and so on. These will broaden your mind and contribute substantially to your professional development. Look for opportunities to attend courses on these topics.

- Model yourself on successful people in your field. Emulate a successful manager within or outside your company. Model their voice, words, gestures, beliefs and attitudes. Practise techniques in coaching/feedback from a credible expert, i.e. someone who is successful and uses the techniques themselves. President Clinton openly admitted that he modelled his presidential style on that of President Kennedy. You can become successful yourself by modelling the success strategies of successful managers.

- Ask a trusted colleague for feedback on your presentation skills, interpersonal relationship skills, meeting skills or work performance. Look for constructive criticism. Remember that mis-

takes are learning opportunities and you can improve outcomes
by reflection and changing your behaviour. However, to do this
you must be aware of your shortcomings.

- Tackle do-it-yourself projects around the house rather than getting others to do it. Take on that repair job yourself. Become
  your own interior designer. Paint and wallpaper your home. Develop PC expertise such as word-processing, spreadsheet analysis, databases, Internet and graphical presentation skills.

- Draw up action plans for work that needs to be done in your job.
  Try to implement things you have learned from books or on
  training programmes.

The VAK Model

VAK is a mnemonic which stands for visual, auditory and kinaesthetic. We learn mostly through these three senses. There are other
senses such as taste and smell, but for our purposes the above three
are the most relevant. Learning experts estimate that we learn 65
per cent through our visual senses; 20 per cent through our auditory senses and 10 per cent through our kinaesthetic senses (from
moving and touching). The VAK model is shown in the following
diagram:

VAK MODEL

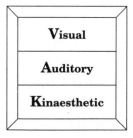

- **Visual learning** might be through videos, CD-ROMs, learning
  maps, graphs and diagrams. Visual learners relate most effectively to written information, notes, diagrams, learning maps
  and pictures. They can remember what they see and reproduce
  it visually. Visual learners like to see the big picture and purpose. At presentations, they like to take detailed notes, even

when notes are provided. Visual learners tend to be best at written communication. They use phrases like "I see what you mean" and "the future looks bright".

- **Auditory learning** might be through reading aloud, asking questions and listening to audio tapes. Auditory learners relate best to the written word. They tend to listen to a lecture, and then take notes afterwards, or rely on handouts. Often written information will have little meaning until it has been heard. For more effective learning, it helps auditory learners to read out loud. Auditory learners may be very good public speakers and they tend to favour professions like law or politics. They have a good ear for accents and can mimic people quite easily. They use phrases like "sounds good to me" and "I hear you loud and clear".

- **Kinaesthetic learners** learn through experience and doing things. Kinaesthetic learning might be through post-it notes, cue cards, exercising while listening to tapes, hands-on approach, role-play and mental rehearsal. Kinaesthetic learners learn effectively through touch and movement and learn skills by imitation and practice. Kinaesthetic learners can appear slow on the uptake if the information is not presented in a style that suits their learning preference. They remember feelings and get an overall impression of a subject. They use phrases such as "I like to get a feel for the situation" and "I must get to grips with the problem".

Mnemonic systems of memory usually assume a visual learning style. Most of the techniques in this book (including mind maps) are aimed at the visual side. If you are an auditory or kinaesthetic learner, this emphasis on imagery may lead to poor recall. If you are an auditory learner, use auditory cues such as sounds to create your mnemonics. If you are a kinaesthetic learner, imagine performing actions in a humorous context as cues for recall.

Good computer packages, especially CD-ROMs, stimulate all three senses. A multi-sensory approach might use the following process:

- Read something and visualise it in your mind. The clearer the images, the more effective the learning.

- Say the key points out loud. Pretend you have to explain it to a friend.

- Write it down, expressing it in your own words. This process engages the kinaesthetic sense, through the actual process of writing and the sensations involved.

- Form a learning set and discuss the issues with a colleague.

- Review the learning just before going to sleep.

- Review the learning again on waking.

The VAK Four Learning Styles

1. The Visual/Verbal learning style

2. The Visual/Non-verbal learning style

3. The Tactile/Kinaesthetic learning style

4. The Auditory/Verbal learning style.

The Visual/Verbal Learning Style

- You learn best when information is presented visually and in written form.

- You prefer to learn with the help of key points or outlines.

- You like textbooks and lecture notes.

- You like to study on your own.

- You like to visualise things in your "mind's eye" when learning.

Learning Strategies for the Visual / Verbal Learner

- Use learning maps to learn new information. Use different colour highlighter pens to emphasise important issues.

- Use cue cards to summarise key information and diagrams that you are learning. Use highlighter pens to make important issues stand out.

- Write out explanatory information for diagrams or models that you want to learn.

- Convert mathematical or technical information into your own words.

- Input your notes into your computer and print out a copy for review.

- Use "post-it" notes for key words and concepts that you need to learn. Put these in places that you will see them. Use this approach coming up towards exams.

The Visual/Non-verbal Learning Style

- You learn best from visual information such as videos, films, pictures, charts, diagrams, graphs, maps and models.

- In a formal learning situation, you prefer facilitators to use visual methods of presentation such as overhead transparencies or slides.

- You prefer textbooks that are illustrated by visual means such as pictures, charts and diagrams.

- You prefer to study on your own rather than in groups.

- When trying to learn new information, you visualise the items in your head.

- Your right brain is highly developed and you enjoy things related to the visual arts and design.

- You use phrases like "I see what you mean".

Learning Strategies for the Visual / Non-verbal Learner

- Make cue cards of key points that you want to learn. Illustrate your cards with cartoons, diagrams and models. Use colour coding to emphasise points. Limit the number of points on each cue card so that you can easily take a mental picture of the content.

- Use visual means such as diagrams, charts and graphs to learn mathematical or technical information.

- Use block diagrams to learn a problem-solving sequence.

- Use your word-processing, database and spreadsheet programs on your computer to organise your learning material.

- When learning written information, convert the ideas into symbols, diagrams or charts.

The Tactile/Kinaesthetic Learning Style

- You have a "hands-on" approach to learning.

- In a formal learning situation, you prefer to be actively involved in doing things such as role-play, simulations, exercises, case studies, discussion tasks and brainstorming sessions.

- You prefer facilitators who use live demonstrations, give classroom problems to solve, and give you projects or assignments to work on in your own time.

- You use phrases like "I like to get a feel for the situation."

Learning Strategies for the Tactile/Kinaesthetic Learner

- In a formal learning situation and to keep you concentrated, sit near the front of the room and take notes such as learning maps.

- Illustrate your learning map with symbols, pictures, diagrams, charts and colour coding.

- When learning, walk up and down with your notes or cue cards and say the information out loud.

- Think of different ways in which you can have a "hands-on" approach to learning. Summarise key information in a learning map. Make a cardboard model of something that you are trying to learn. When studying, take frequent notes and do plenty of problem-solving exercises. If you are studying management, visit an organisation, observe what is going on and talk to senior managers.

- Arrange your cue cards in different sequences. Practise putting the cards in order so that the sequence becomes automatic. Use different coloured highlighting pens to emphasise important points. Bring your cue cards around with you and study them during spare moments of the day.

- When reviewing new information, copy key points on an A3 sheet and hang it on the wall.

- Use the keyboard of your computer to reinforce information by the sense of touch. Organise your information on databases, spreadsheets and word-processing programs and print out for review.

- While walking, listen to audio tapes on your personal stereo. Make your own tapes for important areas of learning.

The Auditory/Verbal Learner

- You learn best when listening to information.

- In a formal learning situation, you like listening to lectures and taking part in discussions.

- You like listening to audio tapes.

- When trying to recall information, you can often "hear" it in your head.

- You learn best when interacting and discussing issues with other people.

- You use phrases like "I hear you loud and clear".

Learning Strategies for the Auditory/Verbal Learner

- You like to study with a colleague when preparing for formal exams or you like to study in a study group. At work, you are part of a learning set.

- You like to talk out loud to aid recall when revising.

- Tape-record critical parts of lectures you attend. Record the counter number for key areas so that you can go direct to them for review.

- Build up a library of your favourite management topics on tape and listen to them while commuting to and from work. Tape the content of your learning maps into audio tapes and use them for review.

- Express mathematical or technical problems in your own words. Think through the solution to problems by talking out loud. To learn a problem-solving sequence, write down the steps and then read them out loud.

The Four Stages of Learning

Awareness of how you learn will make you a more competent learner and a more successful manager. All learning involves persistence, determination and disappointments on the way. Psychologists have discovered that there are four stages in learning, which go from unconscious incompetence to conscious incompetence to conscious competence and lastly unconscious competence. The four stages of learning are illustrated in the following diagram:

THE FOUR STAGES OF LEARNING

1. Unconsciously Incompetent (Enthusiastic Learner)	2. Consciously Incompetent (Disillusioned Learner)
4. Unconsciously Competent (Self-contained Learner)	3. Consciously Competent (Self-conscious Learner)

Let's now look at each of these stages in some detail.

Unconscious Incompetence

This is the stage of learning where you don't know that you don't know. You are just not aware of your own level of ignorance and lack of experience. If you've never driven a car, you will have no idea of what is involved. For example, very young children, like my own seven-year-old grandson, often imagine they can drive a car. Their enthusiasm and confidence exceeds their ability. If you have ever given driving lessons, you begin to appreciate just how much you know without realising it. It is very difficult to express it in words. It is tacit knowledge. This is why it is so difficult for an experienced, competent driver, at the unconscious competent level, to train somebody at the unconscious incompetence level.

It is very difficult to make tacit knowledge explicit. The skills have become habitual, automatic responses and are thus very difficult to verbalise, organise and explain consciously. Many a happy marriage has come to grief because one partner has unwittingly agreed to teach the other how to drive without really thinking about how difficult and traumatic it can prove to be. This demonstrates just how much of our everyday actions are done unconsciously with the minimum of conscious awareness on our part. Everyday habits are activated unconsciously.

Conscious Incompetence

This is the stage of learning where you know you don't know. To learn new things, you must move out of your comfort zone. You start to learn how to drive. You become disillusioned and your confidence drops when you see how awkward you are. You feel you would need to be an acrobat to co-ordinate the movements required for steering, clutch, brake and accelerator, while at the same time watching the control dials and the road. This is the stage where you have kangaroo starts and jerky stops, grind the gears, oversteer and generally challenge the patience of your instructor and other road users. You learn most at this time, but need confidence, persistence and determination to take you to the next stage. Motivation, encouragement, goals, action plans and taking responsibility for your own learning will get you there in the end.

Some people get frustrated and lose confidence at this stage and give up. Consider the number of people who start educational programmes, pay their money and shortly afterwards give them up at great financial loss and personal inconvenience. They don't realise that everybody goes through the same stages of the learning curve and experience negative feelings, setbacks, frustrations and difficulties. There is no gain without some pain. Determination will see you through in the end.

Conscious Competence

This is the stage where you can drive the car but you are very self-conscious of the fact. It takes all your concentration and energy. However, your confidence increases in line with your skill. You are proficient but not a master of the art. You may even pass the driving test at this stage, but you must make a conscious effort to reach the required standard. Overconfidence may be a problem, leading to the taking of unnecessary risks. The result of this is a high rate of accidents for newly qualified young drivers, which is confirmed by road accident statistics.

Unconscious Competence

At this stage, you can drive, listen to the radio and converse at the same time. You are a self-contained learner. Some drivers even manage to converse on their mobile phones while driving, although this practice is not recommended and is illegal in some countries. The movements involved in driving the car have become an automatic response. Your unconscious mind has taken over the routine, freeing your mind to concentrate on the rules of the road and the prevailing traffic conditions. Driving has become a habit. However, the problem with habits is that there are bad habits or poor practice as well as good habits. Many a person over the years has unconsciously acquired poor driving habits which may need to be unlearned and replaced by good habits. This process can be facilitated by unlearning stages 4 to 2 and relearning stages 2 to 4 (see unlearning under the UNIT model below).

When I was learning keyboarding skills I was very conscious, reflective and deliberate about striking the keys. After some practice, I knew where the letters were, but was still very conscious about their position on the keyboard. As a result, I was slow and inefficient. Today, I don't consciously know where any of the letters are, and I'm fast and efficient. I can focus entirely on what I want to write and let my fingers do the work automatically.

Lessons from the Four-Stage Model

Expertise in any area of life takes time, determination, persistence and commitment. It will take about 10 years of application and reading before you become an expert in any subject. Learning is a process, not a destination. To learn, you must go from unconscious incompetence to unconscious competence.

The journey of a thousand miles begins with a single step. As soon as you attain mastery, you must keep up-to-date with developments and best practice as well as consolidating and practising your existing skills. If you fail to do so, your knowledge will be forgotten or become out of date. It is a question of using it or losing it. Lifelong learning and continuous self-improvement is the name of the game. The leading professional bodies have taken this concept on board through their continuing professional development programmes, which are mandatory in some institutes.

The UNIT Model of Learning

The four types of learning can be recalled by the mnemonic UNIT, which stands for Unlearning, New Learning, Incremental Learning and Transformational Learning. Knowing about these will help you to understand and categorise the types of learning you are currently involved in. The UNIT model of learning is shown in the following diagram:

TYPES OF LEARNING

| Unlearning |
| New Learning |
| Incremental Learning |
| Transformational Learning |

- **Unlearning**. It is often harder to unlearn than to learn. These days, many old ways of doing work have to be unlearned and replaced by new ways. The old learning habits die hard and often interfere with our new learning. When changing your old car for a new model, you often have to unlearn old habits and learn new ones to operate improved controls and layouts. With PCs, new and updated programmes come out all the time. Often, previously learned commands for old versions, which have gone into our long-term unconscious memory, give new unexpected results or indeed new commands must be learned to get the same results. Most of us are reluctant to unlearn what we know. In unlearning, you must drop existing knowledge which is now redundant to make room for something new. Psychologists use desensitisation and behavioural therapy programmes to help people unlearn destructive habits and substitute more appropriate behaviour. Managers are sometimes taught behaviour modification methods so they can understand why some employees have learned inappropriate behaviours on the job. The managers then create new environmental experiences for employees that increase the rate of appropriate behaviours or eliminate inappropriate and replace them with appropriate behaviours.

- **New Learning**. In new learning, you will go from a state of unconscious incompetence to a state of unconscious competence. You will go through an "S" curve of progress where, after an initial slow period of learning, you will make rapid progress until you come to a plateau. At this point, it is important to stick to the task, as eventually you will progress to a higher plain of learning. New learning is hard work and requires determination and persistence for success. Repetition and practice is needed to consolidate the new learning. For example, learning keyboarding skills requires putting together many skilled finger movements and combinations. These movements are guided by the letters or word that we want to input. At first, you have to input letter by letter. With practice, you learn to input word by word or phrase by phrase. In verbal learning, such as memorising a poem, we learn sequences of words. We then combine these sequences into an organised whole. Such learning requires much practice and we must overlearn if we want to become truly proficient. Overlearning is learning beyond the stage that you feel you know the topic. Psychologists believe new learning can benefit from old learning because of three factors:

a) Positive transfer of learning. Suppose you learn two tasks. If task two is easier to learn after task one, then positive transfer has occurred. However, if task two is more difficult to learn after task one then negative transfer has occurred.

b) General principles that we learn in one task and apply to another task.

c) Good learning habits that we learn in one task will help us learn another.

- **Incremental Learning**. This means building on your existing learning. For example, you may be fairly competent in making presentations. Many people stop here and don't bother to pursue excellence. However, you can always improve by adopting an attitude of continuous improvement. There is always room for doing better and there is always more to learn about any particular job. Maybe the organisation of your presentation could be improved by having a better introduction and a more positive conclusion. In between, you might use your tone, pitch and delivery to create interest and variety. Being competent in one Windows-based software package means you can transfer the knowledge to another Windows-based package and learn it quite easily.

- **Transformational learning**. This occurs when you solve a problem by understanding the relationships of various parts of the problem. It may occur suddenly, such as when you look at certain problem for some time and then suddenly grasp its solution. A similar type of experience is called a paradigm shift. This is possibly the most important type of learning, because it changes your whole perspective, system of beliefs and attitudes. In creative thinking, it is the "Aha!" experience when you suddenly see things in a different light. For example, you may see your job as a great source of satisfaction rather than a mere source of money. Galileo's discovery, published in 1632, which confirmed the Copernican theory, that the sun, not the Earth was the centre of the universe and that the Earth moved around the sun and not vice versa, is a good example of a paradigm shift. In modern times, business process re-engineering is a radical redesign of business processes to achieve dramatic improvement in productivity and efficiency. It is planned transformational learning.

Lessons from the UNIT Model

Unlearning old ways of doing things and learning new methods is part and parcel of modern living. The old learning often interferes with the new learning, but with practice this will fade away.

New learning goes through the natural stages of unconscious incompetence to unconscious competence. Nothing worthwhile is learnt overnight, so be prepared for the long haul!

Incremental learning is possibly the most common type of learning we engage in. It is also linked to the idea that nothing stays still and we need to continually update and improve our skills. Vegetate and you die.

Transformational learning is radical and the type of learning that you need sometimes to cope with discontinuous change. People often have to go through changes of belief, culture, attitude and skills training in order to progress. Information technology changes and business process re-engineering often give rise to the need for transformational learning.

Learning from Experience at Work

Mumford found that there were four ways of learning from experience at work. The mnemonic PAIR can be used to help you remember the four ways. This is illustrated in the following diagram:

LEARNING FROM EXPERIENCE AT WORK

Prospective
Learning

Accidental
Learning

Intuitive
Learning

Retrospective
Learning

- **Prospective learning**. This is learning from future planned events. It is a type of proactive learning. You are thinking of future events as learning opportunities. How can I learn from future activities? This includes planned management development, on-the-job and off-the-job. On-the-job events might include forthcoming meetings, appraisals, projects, secondments, negotiations and presentations (see Chapter 10). Off-the-job could include training courses, reading assignments, academic courses and using a corporate learning centre (see Chapter 11). Before you go on a formal training programme, you should do some preparation for the anticipated learning, including formulating your learning goals and visualising learning outcomes. Envisage the future and then make it happen. Bill Gates, chairman and chief executive officer of the Microsoft Corporation, dropped out of Harvard in 1977 to pursue full-time his vision of "a computer on every desk and in every home". Much of Gates's success rests on his ability to translate technical visions into market strategy and to blend creativity with technical acumen. Today, most modern inventions and discoveries take place in large research organisations funded by universities, government agencies, private industries, or privately endowed foundations. This is in fact a type of planned and deliberate learning.

- **Accidental learning**. Also called incidental learning, this happens by chance. It is unplanned learning, or learning from mistakes. Accidental learning is followed by reflection. William Conrad Roentgen discovered X-rays accidentally while experimenting with cathode rays. Alexander Fleming (1881–1955), who discovered penicillin, made the first breakthrough by accident. During his work, he noticed an unusual mould growing on a neglected culture dish. He could have ignored this as of little consequence. However, he worked further with the mould and this led directly to the discovery of penicillin.

- **Intuitive learning**. This is where you learn unconsciously from experience. It is learning without reflection. Learning happens inevitably from having experiences. We are learning all the time, whether we are aware of it or not. It is a natural outcome of experiences.

- **Retrospective learning**. This means reviewing and learning from past events. This type of learning is conscious and intentional. Something happens, it is reviewed and lessons are drawn from it. How can I learn from the past? Keeping a learning log is a great way of systematically reviewing the past and learning from it. Necessity and frustration is often the spur to learning and the mother of invention. Fraze Ermal Cleon (1913–1989) had to resort to a car bumper to open a can. After reflecting on the problem for some time, he invented the ring-pull on drink cans.

Lessons from the PAIR Model

Probably the best source of learning is on-the-job experience — the activities and problems faced by managers everyday. Often the missing ingredient is review and reflection. It would be more effective if on-the-job experience became part of a planned management development process rather than leaving it solely to chance. A manager's development needs should be identified and met by a mixture of on-the-job and off-the-job experiences. It is important that these are co-ordinated and planned.

Keeping a learning log is a practical way of implementing retrospective learning. Anticipating learning outcomes and formulating learning objectives in advance is a way of implementing prospective learning. Become conscious of accidental learning so that opportunities are exploited as they arise. We are learning machines. Intuitive learning happens all the time.

The Learning Model

David Megginson developed his model after reflecting on the fact that he was good at reacting to opportunities rather than creating opportunities for himself. The following is Megginson's model:

THE LEARNING MODEL

		Low	High
Planned Learning	*High*	Warrior	Sage
	Low	Sleeper	Adventurer

Low   *High*

Learning from Experience

Planned learning means that learners take responsibility for the direction and control of their training and development. Learning from experience means that learners respond to their experience in a thoughtful and reflective way. There are four types of learner highlighted in the model:

- **Sleepers**. Sleepers show little initiative or response to their experiences. They are low on planned learning and low on learning from experience. They lack an awareness of the need to exploit job activities as learning opportunities. They are ineffective learners. Sleepers have much to learn from warriors and adventurers.

- **Warriors**. Warriors plan their experiences but tend not to learn from them. This is due to a lack of review and reflection on their learning. Because of this they tend not to learn from their mistakes. We describe planned learners as warriors because they have focus, direction, clarity and persistence but lack insight on their learning.

- **Adventurers**. Adventurers respond to and learn from opportunities that come their way but tend not to create opportunities for themselves. This is due to a lack of planned or prospective learning. We call emergent learners adventurers because they have curiosity, flexibility and opportunism, and because they live in the here and now. Adventurers are thus reactive rather than proactive.

- **Sages**. The sage is the ideal learner. Sages both plan and learn from their experiences. Sages have personal development plans and an integrated approach to on-the-job and off-the-job training. Sages have the qualities of warriors and adventurers. They realise that formal and informal learning are complementary and that both are essential to long-term management development.

Barriers to Learning

Some of the barriers to learning can be recalled by the mnemonic RESTATE, which stands for **R**esources, **E**nvironment, **S**tyle, **T**ime, **A**ttitude, **T**raining and **E**xperiences.

- **Resources**. These include a deficit of personal resources such as self-esteem, self-belief and IQ, and organisational resources such as a culture for learning and facilities such as a corporate learning centre or an educational support scheme.

- **Environment**. An environment which does not support learning. A bureaucratic culture inhibits rather than supports learning.

- **Style**. Adopting an inappropriate style will hinder learning. If you are a visual learner, feed your visual senses using videos, CD-ROMs and other visual learning media.

- **Time**. Any worthwhile learning takes time. Insufficient time will create tension and frustrate learning. You need to be in a relaxed state to learn effectively.

- **Attitude**. Negative attitudes will evoke negative outcomes. Self-esteem and self-belief are needed for successful learning.

- **Training**. The training is presented without the needs of the adult learner in mind or the training is irrelevant. Many people are sent on courses because it is their turn or budgetary resources need to be used up before the year-end.

- **Experience**. The learner has insufficient experience or knowledge to make the links and associations necessary for effective learning.

Learning Laws

Newton's insight might be useful to recall here: "Simple laws explain complicated things." The learning laws can be recalled by the mnemonic DEEP AIR, which stands for:

- **Disuse (Law of Disuse)**. If you don't practise a skill or recall and rehearse knowledge, it will eventually be forgotten. Forgetting has nothing to do with age. It's just a consequence of not reviewing. The forgetting curve is a well-established and proven theory in learning. The period immediately following the learning process is the most important time for reinforcing knowledge. You should draw up a review schedule, with reviews about ten minutes after the learning event, after 24 hours, after 1 week, after 1 month, after 3 months and occasionally thereafter to revise and prevent the natural process of decay. Reflect frequently in order to consolidate and integrate new learning with existing knowledge and experience. Learning maps, which concentrate on essentials, should form part of your review plan.

Remembering can be enhanced threefold by using all the senses
— visual, auditory and tactile.

- **Effect (Law of Effect)**. You are more likely to learn and pursue your learning on a longer-term basis if you find the learning
process pleasant, satisfying, enjoyable and rewarding. In formal
learning situations, people often give up learning because of
past unpleasant associations, like being made to feel inadequate
by trainers or educators. Adult learners need all the encouragement, reassurance and support that they can get. Remember
the term "information overload"? If you try to cover too much in
one study session, you will become confused. Concentrate on the
essentials, rather than clouding the issue with too much detail.
Take frequent breaks for rest, review and reflection. Be aware
of your biorhythms. People are usually more alert in the morning, while in the afternoon they tend to be more sluggish, before
they pick up again.

- **Exercise (Law of Exercise)**. The more often you do something, the more proficient you will become. Practice makes perfect — if the practice is the right kind. Doing something the
wrong way can become a habit that you may find hard to unlearn, so make sure you are doing it the right way. In school,
you learned your alphabet and arithmetic tables through repetition or overlearning, until they went into your long-term memory. Now your recall of these is automatic. Similarly, the
operations involved in driving a car, after a period of time, become an automatic response which you do without thinking
leaving, your mind free to attend to other matters as you drive.

- **Primacy (Law of Primacy)**. New things or things that you do
first are remembered better. This is the novelty concept at work.
Likewise, you remember that which is unique and outstanding.
Also, actions that you do last are more lasting. In-between
things are more inclined to be forgotten. When learning a new
subject, you can capitalise on this principle by consciously increasing your powers of observation and concentration during
the early and later stages of the process and actively engaging
all your senses, including writing and doing during the process.

- **Association (Law of Association).** Adult learners learn by linking and associating new knowledge to prior knowledge and existing experience. Association is therefore the basis for most of our learning. Techniques like learning maps, previewing and the SQ3R method act as advance organisers by facilitating the acquisition of new concepts, knowledge and information.

- **Intensity (Law of Intensity).** If you make the learning experience dramatic, interesting, exciting and memorable, it is more likely to be remembered than if it is routine and boring. Consider for a moment what you remember about your holidays. Very little, except the unique, outstanding and funny incidents. The greater and more intense your interest, the more effective the learning is going to be.

- **Readiness (Law of Readiness).** Unless you are innately motivated to learn, your best efforts will be to no avail. You must identify the relevance of the topic, how it relates to your experience and goals and how it can be used to improve on-the-job learning.

The Nine Cs of Learning

Clarity

Effective learning is goal-driven. All successful learners have goals. Training events are guided by training objectives and learning outcomes. Learning goals give you direction and purpose. Concentrate on the end result (where you want to be) rather than the process and difficulties of achieving it. It is the prospect of achieving a clearly defined goal that will mobilise your enthusiasm and commitment. See yourself as being successful with the benefits that will ensue as a result of your success. The self-fulfilling prophecy suggests that you achieve what you expect to achieve and live up to your own and others' expectations. Henry Ford had the goal of producing an affordable car for the masses. All great business ventures and scientific discoveries are driven by goals and clear outcomes.

Curiosity

All great learning and discoveries are preceded by curiosity. Children are naturally curious. However, our regimented educational system seems to kill the curiosity in us. We actively discourage children from asking questions. Adults become embarrassed when confronted with questions like: "Why is the sky blue?" We probably don't know the answer so our response is, "Don't be asking such silly questions." Consequently, as you grow older this natural childlike curiosity is stymied. To become successful learners, you must rediscover and rekindle your natural curiosity for knowledge and learning. Some of the most amazing discoveries in history were prefaced by the word "Why?" Seeking out answers to questions, rather than passively waiting for others to do the thinking for us, is an active form of learning. Edward Jenner (1749–1823) was an English physician who pioneered vaccination. In Jenner's day, smallpox was a major killer. Jenner's curiosity was aroused when he observed that people who worked with cattle and contracted cowpox from them never subsequently caught smallpox. His vaccination giving immunity to smallpox was a great medical breakthrough. Jean Piaget (1896–1980) was responsible for the most comprehensive theory of intellectual development. While working in Binet's Paris laboratory, his curiosity was aroused by the errors children make in intelligence tests. This was the catalyst that led him to study the development of logical thinking. Piaget's ideas about the stage-like development of a child's intellect and discovery-based learning have been influential in education and the design of curricula.

Confidence

Confidence is the belief that you have the innate ability to learn in formal and informal situations. On the other hand, lack of confidence is synonymous with self-doubt, negative attitudes and self-imposed psychological limitations. Self-confidence is the first requisite to great undertakings. Build on your strengths and work to eliminate your weaknesses. Think about the successes you've had in life rather than the failures. See mistakes as learning opportunities and threats as opportunities.

Creativity

Creativity is creating something that wasn't there before; combining things in unique and unusual ways and seeing novel relationships between things, ideas and people. Creative people are not afraid to try out new things and learn from their mistakes. In management, creativity is needed to solve day-to-day problems, come up with unique solutions and insights, design new systems and procedures and develop new products and services. Learning to use the Internet in a creative way is one of the greatest opportunities facing management today. R. Buckminster Fuller (1895–1983) was an American architect, engineer, inventor and poet. He developed the geodesic dome, a large dome that can be set directly on the ground as a complete structure. He was one of the most creative and original thinkers of the twentieth century. As a cartoonist and a master of motion picture animation, Walt Disney (1901–1966) made the world fall in love with a big-eared mouse (Mickey Mouse), a scheming duck (Donald Duck) and many other characters. To children the world over, he is perhaps the greatest and most creative genius of all.

Commitment

According to Disraeli, "the secret of success is constancy to purpose". Persistence is the trait that often sees people through in the end. Abraham Lincoln (1809–1865) spent less than a year in school, but he never stopped studying. He was a lifelong learner. Born in a log cabin, qualified as a lawyer, he became the president who kept the United States united. He is reputed to have given the following advice to a young law student: "Get the books . . . and study them until you understand them in their principal features. . . . Your own resolution to succeed is more important than any other thing." Thomas Edison (1847–1931) inventor of the electric light bulb and phonograph and holder of 1,069 US patents said that genius was 99 per cent perspiration and 1 per cent inspiration. Obstacles often act as a spur to greater learning and achievement. Renoir (1841–1919) the great French impressionist painter, began to suffer from rheumatism in the 1890s. By 1912, he was confined to a wheelchair. Nevertheless, he continued to paint until the end of his life. In his last years, he also took up sculpture, directing assistants to act as his hands.

Conviction

Conviction is the belief that you can do it. We need self-belief if we want to succeed in our careers. To some people, however, recognition does not come in their lifetime. Gandhi (1869–1948) though one of the gentlest of men, had great determination which won independence for India from British rule without striking a single blow. He was a man of very strong convictions who believed that social and political progress could be achieved through peaceful means.

Celebration

Occasionally, you need to pat yourself on the back. Celebrate your little successes and completions. This is a type of reward and reinforcement. This will create positive feelings and give you encouragement to go forward relaxed and determined in the future. Build on your success.

Co-operation

Co-operation here means learning sets and team learning. Having a group of other learners to support and challenge you is a great incentive to learn. Synergy is the idea that two heads are better than one. Teams usually come up with more and better ideas than a person operating alone. Members of a team can share experiences and learn from each other. Research and development teams are set up to develop new products or design new processes. Many major breakthroughs in modern technology have been achieved by people working in teams.

Concentration

Concentration is learning how to cope with, manage and eliminate distractions. Use creative visualisation to get rid of irrelevant thoughts, concerns, daydreams and negative feelings. Visualise yourself learning successfully. Psyche yourself up to the learning task by saying to yourself "My concentration is very sharp"; "I am fully concentrated"; "Every day in every way my concentration gets better and better". Nothing will focus your concentration better than the actual process of beginning the learning task. Newton's most famous work, the *Principia Mathematica* (1687), is often said to be the single most important book published in science. When he was asked how he made the astonishing discoveries in the book, he replied "By thinking on it continually." Michelangelo (1475–1564) was a sculptor, painter and architect. He was a man of genius comparable to the great Leonardo da Vinci. Michelangelo had a remarkable ability to concentrate his thoughts and energy on the task at hand. Often while working, he would eat very little, would sleep on the floor beside his unfinished painting or statue, and continue to wear the same clothes until his work was finished.

Learning through Motivation

Motivation is probably one of the most important factors in successful learning. People must *want* to learn. The DREAM model explores the motivation issue. This mnemonic stands for:

- **Desire**. You must really want to learn.

- **Relevance**. The learning must be relevant to your goals, career and needs. You must identify where the learning can be used to improve your on-the-job performance.

- **Expectation**. You must expect that the learning will meet your needs.

- **Anticipation**. You must anticipate the outcomes of the learning by visualising the positive results and rewards. Mentally rehearse these in your mind's eye.

- **Motivation**. You must be intrinsically motivated to achieve. Intrinsic motivation comes from within. This may be strengthened by extrinsic motivation such as the encouragement or expectations of others.

Summary

Being aware of your learning style can help you become a better learner. The learning cycle is: you do something, you think about it, you make sense of it and then you do it differently. The TRAP model for different types of learners was highlighted. TRAP stands for:

- **T**heorist
- **R**eflector
- **A**ctivist
- **P**ragmatist.

Another approach to learning styles looks at visual, auditory and kinaesthetic learners. This model identifies four styles as follows:

- Visual/Verbal learning style
- Visual/Non-Verbal learning style
- Tactile/Kinaesthetic learning style
- Auditory/Verbal learning style.

Mumford classifies on-the-job experience as intuitive, incidental, retrospective and prospective. The various types of learning can be recalled by the mnemonic UNIT. This stands for:

- **U**nlearning
- **N**ew learning
- **I**ncremental learning
- **T**ransformational learning.

The Laws of Learning can be recalled by the mnemonic DEEP AIR, which stands for:

- **D**isuse
- **E**ffect
- **E**xercise
- **P**rimacy

- **A**ssociation
- **I**ntensity
- **R**eadiness.

The nine Cs of learning were discussed. These are:

1. **C**larity of goals
2. **C**uriosity
3. **C**onfidence
4. **C**reativity
5. **C**ommitment
6. **C**onviction
7. **C**elebration
8. **C**o-operation
9. **C**oncentration

The DREAM model explores the importance of motivation in learning. This stands for:

- **D**esire
- **R**elevance
- **E**xpectation
- **A**nticipation
- **M**otivation.

CHAPTER 2 LEARNING MAP

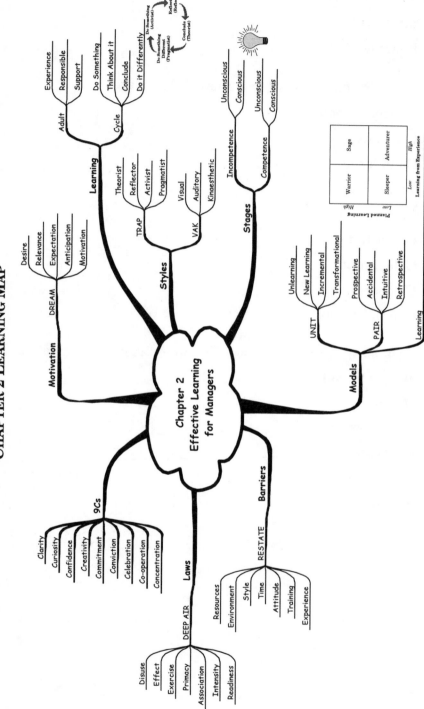

3

Improving Learning IQ

"Anyone who stops learning is old, whether at twenty or
eighty. Anyone who keeps learning stays young.
The greatest thing in life is to keep your mind young."
— Henry Ford

♦ *What are the seven intelligences and how can I improve them?*

♦ *What is emotional IQ?*

♦ *What are managerial competencies?*

♦ *How can I identify, design and evaluate my training?*

♦ *What are the secrets of successful learners?*

♦ *What are the psychological factors in learning?*

The Seven Intelligences

Some people are very quick at learning new things. Some people
have very good memories. Some people are good at solving problems while others are good at learning new words or a foreign language. Some people are good at understanding ideas while others
are good at doing physical tasks. We are all intelligent in our own
unique way. The challenge is to find the way.

The difference between successful learners and average learners
seems to be the extent to which successful learners are able to build
up particular abilities, often by sheer enthusiasm, application, will-

power, effort and years of training. Also, they are often helped by being in the right place at the right time.

In his book *Frames of Mind* (1984), Howard Gardner gives seven reasons to boost your self-esteem for learning. He identifies seven different types of intelligences which we all have to a lesser or greater degree. He defines intelligence as an ability to solve a problem or make a product that is valuable in at least one culture or community. The seven intelligences can be recalled by the mnemonic SIMILAR which stands for **S**patial, **I**nterpersonal, **M**usical, **I**ntrapersonal, **L**inguistic, **A**nalytical or logical, and **R**eflex or movement abilities. This model is shown in the following diagram:

THE SEVEN INTELLIGENCES

Spatial
Interpersonal
Musical
Intrapersonal
Linguistic
Analytical
Reflex

Spatial

People with spatial intelligence are good at objects, shapes, charts, diagrams, pictures and maps. They can visualise maps in their heads and thus have a well developed sense of direction. Well-known examples of people with spatial intelligence would include Pablo Picasso, Rembrandt, Leonardo da Vinci and Michelangelo. People with this ability are excellent at visualisation and think and remember things in the form of pictures. Designers, graphic artists, architects and navigators have this ability. To enhance this ability, use learning maps, diagrams, graphs, flow charts and your powers of visualisation. Of course, successful people with this innate ability working in the professions have, in addition, long years of training and practice behind them.

Interpersonal

These people are good at interpersonal relationships and understanding the motives of others. They have a good sense of empathy and get along very well with people. They are good at interpreting body language and picking up hidden agendas. Many famous people were handicapped in their personal lives by a lack of interpersonal skills. Isaac Newton (1642–1727) had one of the best analytical brains of all time but was an arrogant and difficult man who fell out with many of the other great scientists of the day. Similarly, Albert Einstein's personal life was not very happy. Raphael (1483–1520), unlike his two famous contemporaries, Leonardo da Vinci and Michelangelo, was not a solitary genius but a sociable and approachable figure. Beethoven (1770–1827) had a low interpersonal intelligence. He had a brusque and often uncouth manner. His personal eccentricities and unpredictability were to grow, principally because of his discovery in 1798 that he was going deaf. On the other hand, well-known modern examples of people with good interpersonal intelligence include President Clinton and TV personalities Oprah Winfrey and Terry Wogan. They tend to be extroverts. Interpersonal intelligence is highly prized by employers and is something that is not covered in conventional exams. Salespeople, trainers and human resource specialists such as interviewers, counsellors and negotiators need this ability to survive in their jobs. To enhance this ability, get involved in teams, debating societies, teach others, engage in small talk with shop assistants and socialise as much as possible.

Music

Mozart obviously enjoyed this ability to an exceptional degree. Most of us exercise this talent to a lesser extent by listening to music, having a sense of rhythm and singing along to a tune. Composers, songwriters, musicians and pop artists have this ability. Many people think in music. Beethoven, Elton John, The Beatles, Frank Sinatra and Elvis Presley would be prime examples. To enhance this ability, relax to music and study or read to Baroque music playing softly in the background.

Intrapersonal

People who have this intelligence have self-knowledge and understand their own feelings, strengths and weaknesses. Without self-knowledge people often make very poor decisions in their personal lives with serious consequences. Jung classified people as introverts or extroverts. People with intrapersonal intelligence tend to be introverts. In the learning styles model, they are called reflectors. They tend to be introspective, focusing on inner feelings and intuitions. Monks and others in the religious life, through a contemplative lifestyle, tend to have developed this ability to a high degree. Freud's science of psychoanalysis emerged from his great capacity for introspection. Writers, philosophers and psychologists need this ability to be successful in their careers. Well-known examples would include Plato, Aristotle and Socrates. "Know thyself" was the motto Socrates is reputed to have learned from the Oracle at Delphi. In knowing oneself, he saw the possibility of learning what is really good, in contrast to accepting mere outward appearance. To enhance this ability, reflect on your life's experiences on a daily basis and record them in a diary. Meditation and visualisation would also strengthen this ability.

Linguistic

These are people who are good at reading, writing, talking and languages. They tend to have a good vocabulary, be fluent speakers and good all-round communicators. Your ability in this area is likely to increase right through life and into your 50s, 60s and 70s. Poets, writers, actors, broadcasters, teachers, trainers, preachers and politicians tend to have highly developed linguistic skills. Oscar Wilde (1854–1900) the Irish poet and dramatist, was a great conversationalist and a man of wide learning. James Joyce (1882–1941) the Irish-born author, was one of the greatest literary innovators of the twentieth century. His books contain extraordinary experiments in language and in writing style. Other examples of people with linguistic intelligence are William Shakespeare, Winston Churchill, John F. Kennedy and Bill Clinton. It is not widely known that Winston Churchill, the great English statesman, won the Nobel Prize for Literature. Linguistic intelligence is highly valued in most occupations and in life generally. Many politicians have this ability to a high degree. To enhance this ability, learn from books, tapes, lectures and seminars. Do crosswords and debate issues with friends. Take up part-time lecturing or join Toastmasters.

Analytical or Logical

This intelligence is associated with deductive reasoning. It involves the ability to recognise patterns and to work with abstract symbols and geometric shapes. People with this intelligence are good at logic, problem-solving and doing maths. Accountants, actuaries, engineers, scientists and lawyers are some of the professions that value this ability. Charles Babbage (1792–1871), British mathematician and inventor, who designed and built mechanical computing machines on principles that anticipated the modern electronic computer, had a superb analytical intelligence. In everyday life, people good at household budgeting, organising and time management have this ability. Edward de Bono, of lateral thinking fame, suggests that when looking at problems we should look for plus, minus and interesting factors. Analytical intelligence is usually noticed early in life and peaks at between 30 and 40 years of age. Like linguistic ability, it is highly valued in the academic and business world. To enhance this ability, do mental arithmetic, prepare a cash budget for your personal expenditure and balance your chequebook. To improve your analytical reading skills, operate the PEACE approach which stands for looking for key **P**oints, **E**vidence, **A**ssumptions, **C**onclusions and **E**xamples.

Reflex or Movement

This is also called kinaesthetic or tactile intelligence. Athletes, racing drivers, dancers, mime artists and gymnasts all have tactile intelligence. Surgeons and the skilled trades also need this ability. Surgeons need fine-tuned tactile skills to carry out precise operations and skilled tradespeople need highly developed manual skills. US golfer Tiger Woods stunned the golfing world by winning three consecutive amateur golf tournaments and two professional tournaments by the age of 20. He is an example of outstanding tactile intelligence. Despite the pressures of early stardom, Woods maintains a friendly, down-to-earth presence on and off the links, demonstrating a high interpersonal intelligence. Other well-known examples would include Thomas Edison, Michael Flatley, Fred Astaire, George Best, Charlie Chaplin and Muhammad Ali. People with this ability have a hands-on approach and tend to be mechanically minded. Experiential learning enhances this ability. The action learning approach to management development uses this intelligence. Role-play, to act out what you are learning, will also use this intelligence. To enhance this ability, take notes, make models, learn on the job and practise. The importance of practice to success was emphasised by Gary Player, the famous golf player, who is reputed to have said "The more I practise the luckier I get."

Lessons from the Seven Intelligences

The theory of multiple intelligences is a cause for celebration and high self-esteem. It seems we all have plenty of ability, if only we make the commitment and action plans to exploit our unique talents. You can integrate the seven intelligences into your self-development and continuous improvement plan. When studying, you can summarise your work in the form of learning maps, flow charts and diagrams. This is an application of spatial intelligence. You can discuss issues in groups or get involved in project work. This is an example of interpersonal intelligence. You can relax to your favourite music. This is an example of musical intelligence. Inventing jingles and rhymes to help you remember critical issues is another example.

Reflecting on your work on a daily basis is an example of intrapersonal intelligence. Can you learn from your mistakes and would you do things differently in the future? Keeping a learning log would be a formal way of reviewing. Better still, get involved in a learning set that systematically goes through the learning cycle. This includes reviewing and reflecting on actions taken at work, sharing experiences, drawing conclusions and trying out new ideas.

Writing and making presentations to other managers is an example of linguistic intelligence, as is brushing up on your French and German skills by attending night classes. Inventing mnemonics as memory joggers will improve your linguistic intelligence and ability to recall. Getting involved in the preparation of your departmental budgets or flow-charting organisational systems is an application of logical intelligence.

Lastly, the hands-on approach to work, such as developing PC skills and training schemes such as job rotation are examples of the development of tactile intelligence. In your social life, playing sport of any kind will enhance this ability.

We all have the seven intelligences to one degree or another. Analyse your seven intelligences and find opportunities to develop those that at present are under-utilised and that could help you progress further in your career. If you are a member of these professions, jobs such as accountancy and engineering develop your logical skills to a high degree. It might be a good idea to balance these with any opportunities to develop linguistic and interpersonal skills that are essential for general management.

Conventional IQ tests are pen-and-paper tests with a narrow focus. They concentrate on logical and linguistic abilities and are a poor barometer of success in the business world, where other abilities such as hard work, commitment, determination, enthusiasm and creativity are just as important, if not more so. Although creativity and IQ are known to be related, some people with high IQ are not very creative. On the other hand, some people with average IQ can be very creative. IQ tests, which were developed in 1900 by Binet, a French psychologist, gave rise to the notion that intelligence was fixed at birth and that IQ was the sole criterion of intelligence. This is not true. We all have the ability to improve our multiple IQ. Skills can be developed through use. It just takes a lot of concentrated dedication and effort.

The theory of multiple intelligences highlights the need to recognise and value diversity in the range of abilities that people may have. By developing a variety of approaches to learning and recognising individual strengths and weaknesses, our potential for learning and understanding can be enhanced. Some people may have poor linguistic skills. They may be unable to express something in writing but may very well be able to illustrate it by a drawing or diagrams.

Scientists are equally divided about the relative importance of heredity and environment in determining intelligence. Some psychologists emphasise the importance of the environment in determining IQ. Others attach great importance to heredity. It is safe to conclude that both heredity and environment are both critically important in determining intelligence. A person's genetic intelligence potential can only be developed fully in a favourable environment. On the other hand, a favourable environment can only nurture and grow an intelligence that is there already.

Emotional Intelligence

Socrates said, "know thyself", by which he meant that we have to understand our emotions and learn how to control them. We need to temper our emotions with reason. Emotion without reason and control is a recipe for disaster. On the other hand, we don't want to become like Mr Spock in *Star Trek*, who has no emotions but lives by pure reason. A more harmonious balance between reason and emotion would help us lead more productive and fulfilling lives. The key points of emotional intelligence, which are based on Goleman's research, can be recalled by the mnemonic FARCE. This is illustrated in the following diagram:

EMOTIONAL INTELLIGENCE

| **F**eelings |
| **A**ttitude |
| **R**elationships |
| **C**ontrol |
| **E**mpathy |

- **Feelings**. Self-awareness and self-understanding are a crucial part of emotional intelligence. How can we understand other people if we don't understand ourselves? People who know themselves are more in control of their lives and have a sure sense of their identity and self-worth and where they are going in life. Knowing yourself puts you in a better position to understand and empathise with others.

- **Attitude**. Psychologists have defined attitude as an internal emotional orientation that explains the actions of a person. People with a positive attitude can often recover quickly from illness and the ups and downs of life. Negative thinkers find it difficult to shake off feelings of anxiety and doom and gloom. Positive thinkers see weaknesses as potential strengths and threats as opportunities. They see problems as challenges to be overcome and mistakes as learning opportunities.

- **Relationships**. Being good at interpersonal relationships is useful in any occupation, but especially for those who deal a lot with people. These days, managers need to demonstrate good communication, inspirational, leadership and teambuilding skills if they want to succeed in their careers. They must be able to manage difficult employees and handle conflict situations.

- **Control**. Being in control of your emotions means you can postpone gratification and stifle impulsive behaviour. People with out-of-control emotions do things that impact negatively on themselves and others for the rest of their lives. This can range from the trivial, such as antagonising your friends over some small difference of opinion, to murdering the next door neighbour because of a long-standing dispute. In the US, emotionally immature people have massacred schoolchildren for little apparent cause. People with self-control can plan for the future and diligently pursue their goals and dreams with dedicated hard work over long periods of time. They sacrifice the present for future gain. Olympic gold athletes spend years training many hours per day, six days per week, before realising their dreams. They postpone gratification and show tremendous self-control by sacrificing their social life over many years for a dream of Olympic fame. All great sport achievers dream the impossible dream and then make it happen.

- **Empathy**. Empathy is being tuned into other people's feelings. Native Americans have a saying: "Before you criticise and choose, walk a mile in my shoes." These skills are particularly needed in the caring professions, such as religion, nursing and psychology.

Lessons from Emotional IQ

The findings from emotional IQ suggests that you don't need to be a genius to be successful in life. It highlights the importance of a disciplined mind, self-confidence, an even temperament, a positive attitude, and good relationship skills to a happy and successful life. It suggests the need to be in control of your emotions rather than being out of control. Spite, anger, jealousy, hatred, bitterness, sarcasm, resentment and sabotage are just some of the everyday problems encountered in the workplace caused by emotional immaturity. The cost of these to a business, though hidden, can be substantial. On the other hand, emotional competence can make the difference between a business failing and a business succeeding. Emotionally intelligent employees are happy in their work and enjoy good work relationships and job satisfaction.

Conventional measures of IQ, which concentrate on logical and linguistic skills, give less than half the picture. In a work context, emotional intelligence, such as intrapersonal and interpersonal skills, are more important than technical skills. These are the types of skills you need to enable you to learn on the job and go on learning. To learn effectively, you must be able to reflect and learn from setbacks and mistakes rather than getting upset and despondent.

Many of the professions are high on linguistic and logical skills, but ignore the emotional, intuitive and relationship aspects of life skills. Managers need to be aware of the necessity of developing skills in these areas. Coaching, counselling, mentoring, conflict resolution, management by wandering about (MBWA), handling social occasions in the workplace, keeping cool under pressure, listening and negotiating are just some of the emotional IQ skills a manager needs.

Emotional intelligence distinguishes leaders from managers. The higher you go in the organisation, the more important it becomes. Leaders need to keep cool under the most trying circumstances. While the ability to take a strategic view is important for success in senior management, it is emotional intelligence that makes the difference between a great leader and a mediocre performer. Even in low level jobs, people with emotional intelligence are three times as productive as those without this skill.

Practise and reflect on the "FARCE" model if you desire to become proficient in emotional intelligence.

Learning by Objectives

Learning objectives are needed so that you can compare actual results against objectives and take corrective action as needed to reach your goals. Some mechanism of feedback is necessary so that you know when things are going wrong. Learning objectives provide a purpose and a sense of direction. They will help you organise and direct your learning activities. The importance of objectives in successful learning cannot be overstated.

Objectives can be considered under the following headings:

- **Knowledge**. Have you acquired the knowledge that you set out to acquire?

- **Comprehension**. Knowledge without understanding is not very useful. Have you acquired the conceptual framework for the knowledge and do you understand its significance and relevance particularly in the work situation? Practice without theory is blind.

- **Application**. Are you able to apply the knowledge to your general life or work situation? In business you need to have a practical bias. Theory without practice is not very useful.

- **Analysis**. Can you break down the knowledge into its component parts? Chunking is often necessary to achieve understanding.

- **Synthesis**. Can you recombine the component parts of the knowledge so that you are able to grasp the complete picture?

- **Evaluation**. Have you achieved your learning objectives?

The reason you must learn is all-important. Keep the WIIFM principle in mind: "What's in it for me." Consider the personal benefits of learning, your needs and interests.

Learning Needs of Managers

How do you identify managerial skills? Generally, managerial competencies have been identified and researched very well in the literature. These competencies can be studies, learned and practised on the job until a high level of proficiency is reached. Among the best-known empirical studies on what managers actually do are those by Henry Mintzberg, John Kotter, and Rosemary Stewart (see Cole, 1995). Henry Mintzberg identified the key managerial roles as follows:

- **Interpersonal**. Within the interpersonal role, he identified three sub-roles: figurehead, leader and liaison. The figurehead role would include taking important clients to dinner, attending opening ceremonies and making presentations on behalf of colleagues to employees retiring. As a leader, the manager selects, trains and motivates employees. He encourages workers to increase productivity. Liaison would include maintaining contact with customers, suppliers and banks.

- **Informational**. Within the informational role, Kotter identified three sub-roles: monitor, disseminator and spokesperson. As a monitor, the manager actively seeks out information that may be of use to the organisation. He might scan business magazines for information about competitors or new technological developments. As a disseminator, he might spread this information to other parts of the organisation. He might send out memos defining new policies and procedures. As a spokesperson, the manager might represent the company to outsiders at press conferences to announce a new product launch or a new factory planned, or indeed to defend the position of the company.

- **Decision-making**. Within the decision-making role, Kotter identified entrepreneur, disturbance handler, resource allocator and negotiator. The manager as entrepreneur identifies new business opportunities for the company. As a disturbance handler, the manager helps to resolve disputes between employees or between unions and management. As a resource allocator, the manager is responsible for budgets and the allocation of manpower, money, materials and equipment. As a negotiator, the manager is responsible for reaching agreements between major customers, suppliers and unions.

John Kotter found that general managers spend a typical day doing the following:

- They spend most of their time with others, including their own managers and staff

- They have in-depth discussions on a wide range of issues;

- In these discussions, general managers typically ask a lot of questions;

- During these discussions, general managers rarely seem to make significant decisions;

- Discussions include a lot of social banter and non-work-related issues;

- In some of these encounters, the key issues discussed are not important to the business;

- In such encounters, the general managers rarely give "orders" in the traditional sense, but rather seek to influence others;

- In the allocation of time, general managers often react to the initiative of others;

- Most of the time with others is spent in short, disjointed conversations;

- They work long hours, often up to 60 hours per week.

Rosemary Stewart summarises a manager's job broadly as:

- Deciding what should be done and then getting other people to do it;
- Setting objectives;
- Planning (including decision-making);
- Setting up formal organisations;
- Motivation;
- Communication;
- Control (including measurement);
- Developing people.

Fred Luthans, based on observation of real managers at work, lists the activities of managers as:

- Planning and co-ordinating;
- Staffing;
- Training and development;
- Making decisions and solving-problems;
- Processing paperwork;
- Exchanging routine information;
- Monitoring and controlling performance;
- Motivating and reinforcing;
- Disciplining;
- Liaising with people outside the company;
- Managing conflict;
- Socialising and politicking.

In summary, one can see that the following are the key competencies of managers:

- Interpersonal relationship skills;
- Communication skills;

- Problem-solving and decision-making skills;

- Negotiating skills;

- Networking skills;

- Time management skills;

- Planning skills;

- Developing others.

As a manager, you should take every opportunity to acquire these skills by a planned process of on-the-job and off-the-job learning. These days, managers need a portfolio of skills if they want to survive not only in their present jobs, but also in the marketplace generally. Included in that portfolio would be information technology skills and all-round business knowledge.

Designing Personal Development Plans

Having identified your training and development needs, you now need to design a personal development plan to meet your needs. You will probably need to agree this with your manager, but take responsibility for your own learning. Take the initiative. Do not be waiting around for others to do it for you. After all, they are likely to prioritise their own interests rather than yours.

You will also have long-term needs to meet your career aspirations. Your long-term needs may be met through mentoring and attendance at external management development programmes. You might also contemplate doing degree or postgraduate studies. A basic requirement for most management positions now is a third-level qualification. Your personal development plan should include a reading programme to get familiar with current management thinking and the latest management developments.

Evaluating Your Training and Development

Evaluation means assessing whether or not your learning objectives have been met. According to Kirkpatrick, evaluation can be done at four levels, as in the following diagram:

EVALUATION MODEL

- **Reaction**. Do you feel satisfied and happy after the learning experience? Were you happy with the quality of the training?

- **Learning**. Have you learned new skills, attitudes and knowledge? The acquisition of new skills and knowledge can be examined and tested during and after the course programme.

- **Job**. Can you transfer the knowledge and skills to your work situation? General management skills can be transferred over a period of time as the need arises. On the other hand, PC skills can be used straight away.

- **Organisation**. Will the company benefit as a result of your new knowledge and skills? Increases in productivity, efficiency, customer service and sales turnover would be key indicators.

Successful Learning

Interest and commitment is more important for success in life and learning than formal education. Many of the great figures in history had little or no formal education. Let's now examine brief biographical notes on some of the most prominent scientific, historical and literary figures to see what we can learn from their lives:

- **Albert Einstein** (1879–1955) formulated theories about the nature and structure of the universe that totally changed our understanding of how things behave. Isaac Newton's theories had been accepted for 200 years. In 1905, Einstein published his Theory of Relativity. His famous theory is an example of transformational learning. Einstein's reputation for a slowness in learning in his early years came from the fact that he put little effort into things that he was not interested in. When at elementary school, he showed an interest in science and mathematics but did poorly in other subjects. He hated the rigid school system in Germany at the time where the conventional wisdom of the day, as elsewhere in the Western World, was corporal punishment for a wrong answer.

Einstein spent his time in the library reading and researching things that mattered to him rather than attending to his formal studies. As a result, he often had to cram at the last minute to get his college degree. Because of his poor marks, his initial job was at the Swiss Patent Office in Bern. This did not stop Einstein from formulating his theories, which would revolutionise science. Einstein's approach to learning emphasised using and integrating all of the senses. He had great powers of imagination, concentration and visualisation. Einstein's fantasy of himself riding a beam of sunlight played an important part in the discovery of the theory of relativity. He used the right brain to visualise the theory and the left brain to translate it into mathematical symbols.

- **Michael Faraday** (1791–1867), the English physicist and chemist, discovered electromagnetic induction, which led to the electric generator. He had little formal education and was apprenticed to a bookbinder at age 14. He was a self-directed learner and voraciously read all the scientific books in the shop. This proved to be the foundation on which he built subsequent discoveries.

- **Charles Darwin** (1809–1892) was England's greatest biologist. He was such an indifferent student at school that his father declared, "You care for nothing but shooting, dogs, and rat-catching, and you will be a disgrace to yourself and your family." Like Einstein, the young Darwin was interested in things outside the school curriculum. At school he had no interest in classical languages and ancient history. He liked best to collect shells, birds' eggs and coins. He also watched birds and insects and helped his brother make chemical experiments at home. In later years, Darwin maintained that these activities were the best part of his education.

- **Thomas Edison** (1847–1931) had only three months formal education. Because of his very large head, the doctors thought he might have brain trouble. His teachers thought him stupid because he asked so many questions. However, his mother believed in him and encouraged him to read widely. By the age of ten, he had begun to do chemistry experiments and had his own laboratory at home. He was a very industrious youth and by the age of 12 he was selling newspapers.

- **Abraham Lincoln** (1809–1865) spent less than a year in school, but he never stopped studying. He was a lifelong learner. Lincoln's stepmother encouraged him to study. He could never get enough to read. He said: "The things I want to know are in books. My best friend is the man who'll get me a book I haven't read." He was always interested in new things. He became interested in law and studied long hours to qualify as a lawyer.

- **Benjamin Franklin** (1706–1790) was a US revolutionary and statesman. Franklin's formal schooling ended when he was ten and he then trained as a printer. He was a self-taught scientist and inventor who developed, among other things, the lightning conductor and bifocals. He also enjoyed widespread success as a writer and publisher. He was involved in drafting the peace treaty that secured American independence from Britain.

- **Andrew Carnegie** (1835–1919), born in Scotland, became a famous US industrialist and philanthropist. He left school at 14 and became a self-made man. He endowed public libraries, education, and various research trusts.

- **Charles Dickens** (1812–70) was one of England's greatest authors. His basic education consisted of only a few years' secondary education. His real education came from his reading and observation and daily experience. Dickens had a reporter's eye for the details of daily life and a mimic's ear for the subtleties of common speech. Further, he had the artist's ability to select what he needed and shape them into works of lasting value.

- **Helen Keller** (1880–1968) was an American author and lecturer. She is a learning model and inspiration for all people with disabilities. When 19 months old, she was stricken with an acute illness that left her deaf and blind. No one could be found to educate her until her seventh year, when she began her special education in reading and writing with Anne Sullivan. She quickly learned to read by the Braille system and to write using a specially designed typewriter. Ten years later, she went to college and graduated with honours in 1904.

- **Virginia Woolf** (1882–1941), British author and critic, had no formal education. She was educated at home by her father. Nevertheless, she became one of the most prominent writers of the twentieth century. She was one of the leading figures in the literary movement called modernism.

- **Walt Disney** (1901–66) left high school without graduating but went on to win more than 100 prizes for his films, including 29 Academy awards. Like Edison, he was an industrious young boy and did weekly sketches for a barber for a payment of 25 cents or a haircut. His real interest was in art and he took evening courses to develop this talent. Disney's first drawings as a boy were of farm animals. In 1964, he was awarded the Presidential Medal of Freedom.

- **George Bernard Shaw** (1856–1950) was a famous Irish writer. Shaw's formal education did not last very long. He was tutored by his uncle, then attended day schools, in which he was "near or at the bottom" of his class. By the age of 15, he became a clerk in a land agent's office. At 20, he moved to London and spent his days at the British Museum reading room, studying and writing several novels, which were all failures. During the evening, he attended lectures and debates and developed into an excellent public speaker. All this was to lay the foundation for his subsequent success.

Lessons from the Great Learners

- Intense curiosity and interest in a particular area of learning is the driving force for great learners.

- The great learners had the ability to identify their strengths and then exploit them. Mozart knew his strengths and weaknesses. He is reputed to have said: "I am no poet. I cannot distribute phrases with light and shadow; I am not a painter. I am a musician."

- Lack of formal education is not a barrier to great learning. Even today, many individuals who are indifferent scholars often prove very successful in business or the arts. On the other hand, some individuals who excel at school often do very poorly when they leave.

- The great learners learnt by observation, experience, experimentation and reflection. They were creative problem solvers and transformational learners. They often turned their backs on accepted models of their time and formulated their own new models or theories.

- The great learners learnt from their mistakes. Henry Ford said: "Failure is the opportunity to begin again more intelligently." They often turned defeat into opportunities. They did not let the trials and tribulations of life deter them from their mission. In life, they were often misunderstood and held in contempt by peers. To be a successful learner, you must have the ability to handle rejecters.

- Many of the great learners had supportive parents, teachers and mentors who encouraged them in their quest for greater knowledge.

- Wide reading and self-development activities are the habits of great learners.

- The great learners had great powers of concentration and possessed tremendous sources of energy. The importance of dedication and practice in their chosen field is evident. It takes at least ten years to become an expert in a field and then one must work hard to keep up with developments.

- The great learners often had good powers of imagination and visualisation. Many kept diaries similar to learning logs to reflect on their experiences.

- The great learners often excelled in specific areas and often showed little talent in other areas. Freud, the famous psychologist, was poor at mathematics. He said: "I have an infamously low capability for visualising spatial relationships, which made the study of geometry and all subjects derived from it impossible to me." However, he was very gifted in language and understood himself and others. It seems some individuals who have great language skills may have great difficulty with mathematics or science. On the other hand, individuals with great engineering skills often can't put a coherent paragraph together.

- From an early age, many of the great learners were industrious and resourceful.

- The more you stimulate your brain through learning, the better it becomes. Researchers have found that learning increases the number of dendritic connections in the brain.

Other Psychological Factors in Learning

Obviously, psychological factors are very important in determining our success or otherwise as learners. Our minds are influenced by fears, feelings, emotions and attitudes. A mnemonic FEMALE will help you remember some of the key factors involved. This stands for **F**eedback, **E**motions, **M**otivation, **A**ttitude, **L**evel of Stress and **E**steem. Let's now explore each of these:

- **Feedback**. Knowledge of results is feedback on your performance as a learner. A manager who receives timely, accurate and clear feedback from a mentor or senior manager is in a position to learn from experience and take corrective action for the future. It is very hard to improve if you are unaware of where you are going wrong. In practice, many managers do not give any feedback to employees on their performance or do not give feed-

back as often as they should. The normal performance appraisal, held annually or semi-annually in many firms, does not
meet the timely criteria for effective feedback. This would suggest that performance appraisal should be a continuous process
of on-the-job feedback rather than a once-off event. Research
has demonstrated that knowledge of results alone is not likely
to change a person's work habits, but must be tied in with an
individual's goals to be successful. Computer-based training is
built around the concept of objectives, practice and feedback.
The courseware is specially designed to provide reinforcement
by giving plenty of practice. In some courses, learners are not
allowed to progress until earlier stages have been mastered.

- **Emotions**. We are driven by our emotions. All the great learners were emotionally committed to their subjects. If you are enthusiastic and intensely interested in a subject you are more
likely to learn and remember it. On the other hand, anxiety may
inhibit learning. Also, unpleasant experiences may be re-
pressed. The development of memories about unpleasant experiences may develop into continuing fears or phobias. People of
genius are often intense and highly strung with a great drive to
achieve.

- **Motivation**. Motivation may be intrinsic, coming from within,
or extrinsic, coming from without. Intrinsic motivation is the
stronger because it means you want to learn to meet your own
goals rather than the expectations or goals of others such as
parent or peer pressure. However, the expectations of others do
influence motivation. Employees who are set clear goals frequently improve their performance and job satisfaction. High
but realistic expectations are most effective. For example, all
the ingredients for successful learning are often designed into
computer-based training. These include motivational objectives,
learner responsibility and opportunities for feedback of results.
Maslow's hierarchy of needs can be adapted as a motivation
model for learning. At the physical and safety level, a stimulating, secure, supportive and safe environment must be provided
for learning. At the emotional level, the learner must be made

responsible for their learning but at the same time must be given recognition, respect, acceptance and a sense of belonging. At the intellectual level, the learning should be varied, stimulating and challenging. At the self-actualisation level, the learning must be meaningful, provide a sense of purpose and be a vehicle for self-expression and self-development.

- **Attitude**. To be successful in learning, we must have a belief in our capacity for self-improvement and development. What matters most in life is not what happens to us but our attitude towards what happens and how we cope with it. Maintaining the right attitude towards lifelong learning and development means seeking out like-minded people who will support you in the achievement of your goals. A positive attitude to self-development is reinforced by immersing yourself in self-improvement books, tapes, videos and courses in self-improvement. The self-fulfilling prophecy states that you become what you expect to become and you achieve what you expect to achieve, provided of course that you support your goals by action programmes.

- **Level of stress**. An optimum amount of stress will help you in your goals as a learner. Too much stress is a barrier to learning. Social support, as provided in learning sets, may act as an antidote to stress. Relaxation training, such as progressive relaxation or meditation, will help you control stress levels.

- **Esteem**. Self-esteem is the value we place on ourselves. Low self-esteem results in low performance. High self-esteem is crucial to our well-being and our self-development. To be successful learners we must see ourselves as capable and effective learners. People with high self-esteem see threats as opportunities and mistakes as learning opportunities. They engage in positive self-talk and failure is never entertained.

Physical Factors in Learning

- **Attention Span**. Your attention span is unlikely to be more than 20 minutes. In a learning session of one hour, this would suggest that you take mini-breaks every 20 minutes or so. One of the easiest ways to help your attention is to drink sufficient water throughout the day. Dehydration can cause attention difficulties. So take a drink of water during your mini-breaks. Short attention spans seem to be now part of our way of life. For example, the frequent television breaks on American TV are supposedly dictated by the short attention span of many Americans. In contrast, the genius of Newton relied partly on his ability to concentrate on particular problems for very long periods of time.

- **Sleep**. Getting adequate sleep is vital to your success as a learner. Shakespeare called sleep the "balm of hurt minds" and "chief nourisher in life's feast". Lack of sleep affects all activities adversely, but it seems to affect memory more than physical tasks. Lack of sleep, per se, does not interfere with memory. However, tiredness greatly affects your motivation to learn new things, accept new challenges and exercise your memories. It also adversely affects your ability to concentrate. Learning important facts and concepts just before you go to sleep consolidates the learning. It is further strengthened if you review on waking up.

- **Forgetting**. One reason for forgetting is that the information was never registered in the first place. It was never transferred from your short-term memory to your long-term memory. You must overlearn information if you want it to be registered in your long-term memory. A systematic review programme will help you do this. One theory suggests that forgetting is caused by interference or inhibition. In proactive inhibition, old memories interfere with the retention of new ones. In retroactive inhibition, new learning interferes with retention of the old. This theory suggests that there is a balance maintained between input, such as learning, and output, such as forgetting. Obviously, our minds would become overloaded if we remembered everything and prioritising memories would be impossible.

Learning Curves, Cycles and Mental Maps

Learning Curve

You have probably heard the expression "he went through a steep learning curve". The learning curve is in fact a graph that can be drawn to represent the pattern of learning in many production and construction tasks. It is also experienced in other areas of learning, but may be difficult to quantify. In learning, there is usually a rapid advance at the beginning, which then levels out into a plateau, which takes off again before flattening out into another plateau. However, all learning curves do not follow this pattern. Some people may experience very slow progress at the beginning of a learning task. Understanding the nature of learning curves is important for a manager. The obvious message is that the pace of improvement in a skill or a knowledge area is not constant. It will be rapid and dramatic at times and at other times very slow or at a standstill.

In industry, it has been found that the time required to do most tasks of a repetitive nature gets shorter because, as the tasks are done, more and more experience in doing them is built up. In the US aircraft industry, an 80 per cent learning curve was found to apply. This meant that cumulative average time to produce an aircraft fell by 20 per cent for each doubling of output for that type of aircraft. The learning curve has important applications for manufacturing processes. Any change in production schedules and processes initially reduces efficiency because it involves some learning or relearning. For similar reasons, the cost characteristics of new products tend to improve with time as machine speeds, labour efficiency and material usage levels increase as the learning curve affects them. From a personal development point of view, any new learning challenge will have periods of rapid progress, no progress and slow progress. To be a successful learner, you must persist through the periods of no progress and slow progress.

Virtuous and Vicious Learning Cycle

Motivational theory states that behaviour that is not rewarded is unlikely to be repeated. A virtuous learning experience is one where the learning is seen as relevant, is successfully transferred to an on-the-job situation and the outcome is rewarded by recognition of some sort. A vicious learning experience is where the learning is not seen as relevant and is therefore not put into effect. This might lead to a situation where all new learning is seen as irrelevant and not worth the effort. As you grow older, your short-term memory capacity declines and learning becomes more difficult unless you stimulate your mind with new challenges. The combination of these two factors becomes a vicious circle. You are less inclined to exercise your mind with new learning challenges. On the other hand, your failure to develop your brain means you become more resistant to new learning, making it still harder to learn and further demotivating yourself.

Mental Maps

These are personal models of reality — the way you see the world. They are moulded by our experience, beliefs and values. You share aspects of your mental maps with other people, but no two people have identical mental maps. Mental maps are relevant to learning and development. Development can be viewed as a process of changing our mental maps. Transformational learning, similar to paradigm shifts, occur when you radically change your mental map of the world. In negotiation, this might be a change from a win–lose approach to a win–win approach. In leadership, it might be a move from an autocratic to a democratic style. To be an effective communicator, it is important to realise that people do not share common mental maps. Empathy is the ability to get inside another's mental map. In neuro-linguistic programming, they say that the map is not the territory. This means that your map of reality is not reality itself.

Learning through Questions

Pose questions as a tool for learning. Asking the right questions is a great way of learning. The more perceptive, incisive and meaningful the questions the better. William Harvey (1578–1657) was an English physician who discovered the circulation of blood through a process of questioning, experimentation and reflection. He set out to query Galen's account of the threefold circulation of the blood, which was the accepted paradigm of the time and had been for 1,500 years. Questions create a tension between our existing level of knowledge and our desired level of knowledge. Learning abhors a vacuum, which inevitably you will seek to fill.

"What if" questions open up an awareness to choice and possibilities. "Who" questions focus on your identity. "Why" questions focus on your beliefs and values. "How" questions focus on your capabilities. "What" questions focus on your behaviour and "where" and "when" questions on your environment. It is important that you be aware of the level at which you pitch your questions. For example, if I want to improve my PC (personal computer) skills, it would probably be better to ask, "What do I need to do to improve my PC skills?" (behaviour level), rather than "Why am I pretty useless with a PC?" (capability) or worse still, "Who am I and why am I such a useless PC person?" (identity). By contrast, if I sense a lack of motivation to improve my PC skills, then "who" and "why" questions may be more helpful. It may be, for example, that I don't really see myself as a PC person (identity) or that PC skills have a low priority in my life (values).

Crick and Watson discovered the molecular structure of DNA (deoxyribonucleic acid) in 1953 and began a whole new science of molecular biology by asking the right question ("How do genes replicate and carry information?"). Pertinent questions come before all great scientific discoveries.

Summary

The SIMILAR model for multiple IQ was discussed. This stands for:

- **S**patial
- **I**nterpersonal
- **M**usical
- **I**ntrapersonal
- **L**inguistic
- **A**nalytical

- **R**eflex or kinaesthetic.

The important contribution of emotional IQ to overall intelligence was highlighted in the model FARCE:

- **F**eelings
- **A**ttitude
- **R**elationships
- **C**ontrol
- **E**mpathy.

The importance of learning objectives, identifying learning needs, designing personal development plans and evaluating learning was discussed. The characteristics of successful learners were illustrated with short case studies of famous historical and scientific figures.

The psychological factors in learning can be recalled by the mnemonic FEMALE, which stands for:

- **F**eedback
- **E**motions
- **M**otivation
- **A**ttitude
- **L**evel of stress
- **E**steem.

Other factors in learning include virtuous and vicious learning cycles, attention span, sleep, forgetting, the learning curve, mental maps and using questions to stimulate learning.

CHAPTER 3 LEARNING MAP

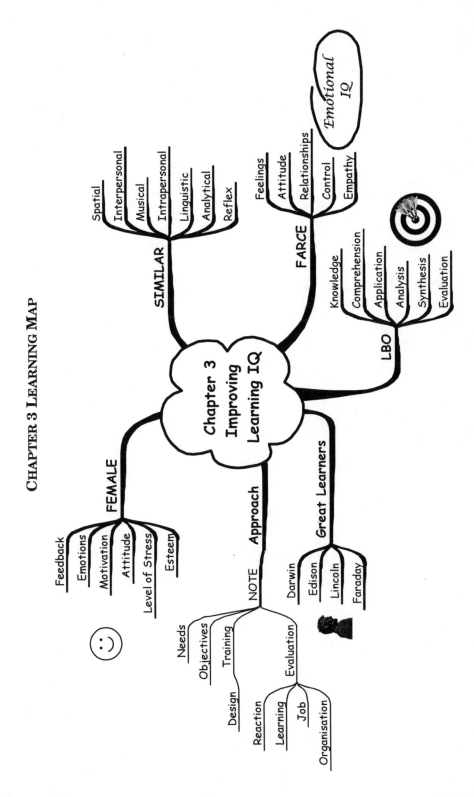

4

The Learning Organisation

*"Learning should be equal to or greater than
the rate of change." — Reg Revans*

♦ *What is a learning organisation?*

♦ *What are the core beliefs of a learning organisation?*

♦ *What are the values of a learning organisation?*

♦ *What can you do to make it happen?*

♦ *What are the conditions that trigger a learning organisation?*

♦ *What are the conditions that inhibit a learning organisation?*

♦ *How can we use models to understand the learning organisation?*

Definition

A learning organisation is an organisation that values learning. The learning organisation makes experience explicit and transforms it into knowledge. It has the flexibility to provide learning where it's needed in the organisation. Learning is an ongoing, rather than a once-off event. In the ideal organisation, every employee is committed to lifelong learning. They want to be better tomorrow than they are today, through learning. The organisation is devoted to continuous improvement of its products, services and processes through learning about learning. Employees will experience better job satisfaction, customers will experience better service and the organisation will build a more prosperous and lasting future for itself.

Core Organisational Beliefs — Learning

- Learning is fun.

- Lifelong learning is encouraged.

- People learn from mistakes. Management by blame is discouraged.

- Learning sets are the norm.

- Reflection is a normal part of learning.

- Learning is integrated into all aspects of the job.

- Learning is accessible to all employees.

- The aim is to create an environment conducive to learning.

- The company believes in whole brain learning.

- Mentoring and coaching are an integral part of management development.

- People are responsible for their own learning.

- There is a bottom-up approach to learning.

- Senior management support learning.

Core Organisational Beliefs — Empowerment

- People are the organisation's most important resource.

- The dignity of the person is sacrosanct.

- Teams are the building bricks of the organisation.

- A win–win approach to negotiations is essential.

- Participation in decision-making is essential.

- A democratic leadership style is essential. Managers should be facilitators rather than directors.

- Open communication between management and staff is essential.

- Information technology is used to inform and empower the many rather than the few.

Core Organisational Beliefs — Attitudes

- Focus on continuous improvement rather than the "one right answer".

- Focus on solutions rather than problems.

- Total quality management.

- Getting it right first time.

- Creativity is encouraged through a questioning approach. Questions stimulate learning.

- The customer is the focus of the business.

- Collaboration rather than competition.

- The company believes in multi-skilling and job flexibility.

Values

A bureaucracy is probably the opposite of a learning organisation. A bureaucracy values stability, precedent and consistency. It hates change. Employees are not encouraged to use their initiative and managers spend much of their time engaged in unproductive organisational politics. On the other hand, the learning organisation encourages its employees to use their initiative and managers to engage in purposeful activity. The values of the learning organisation are thus:

- **Learning**. Employees are trained in learning to learn skills. They are encouraged to be lifelong learners and to take responsibility for their own learning. The organisation realises that learning from mistakes is the most effective form of learning. Human infallibility is accepted and thus the blame culture is discouraged. The organisation encourages and rewards experimentation, different perspectives, exploration of new ideas and creativity. The management facilitates the transfer of knowledge throughout the organisation. A variety of mechanisms may be used, including written, oral and visual reports, site visits and tours, rotation programmes and learning and training programmes. Employees are encouraged to adopt a questioning approach to all aspects of the business. Tensions are welcomed, as they evoke creative solutions to problems that were previously resolved on a "win–lose" basis.

- **Participation** is encouraged at all levels. Employees are empowered to make decisions for their own areas of work activity. They are consulted by management and their views are valued. Management encourage as wide a debate as possible when formulating strategy and policy. Employee directors, quality circles, share ownership, and suggestion schemes are some of the more common methods of participation.

- **Open communication**. Real two-way communication between management and staff is part of the culture. Cross-boundary communication between departments is needed. Empathising or listening with understanding and feeling is encouraged. The cascade system of communication is sometimes used. This is where the chief executive briefs the directors, who in turn brief the senior management team. They in turn brief the next level and so on, until all in the organisation have been briefed. At each level, two-way communication is encouraged and facilitated.

- **Systematic problem-solving**. This is preferred to guesswork, hearsay and "seat of the pants" management. This philosophy draws heavily on the values and methods of the quality movement. It relies on the scientific method rather than guesswork for diagnosing problems. This is what Deming called the "plan, do, check, act" cycle. Fact-based management — insisting on data, rather than assumptions, for decision-making — is the order of the day. Statistical tools are used to organise data and draw conclusions. These would include histograms, Pareto charts, correlations and cause-and-effect diagrams.

- **Customer focus**. The organisation responds around the needs of the customer. Market research is used to identify the needs of customers. The employees must be taught the core value that without the customer the company would not be in business. Customers generate revenue which supports all expenditure and makes profits.

Making it Happen

How do you create the right environment for a learning organisation? Learning organisations don't just happen. You have to make them happen! They also won't happen overnight. Creating a learning organisation is a gradual process, which takes time and patience. The following are some practical things that you can do to make it happen:

- **Decentralisation**. To empower employees, you must put the organisational structures in place. Large companies need to be divided up into strategic business units or divisions. These will have their own management structures and business plans. Within these structures, as much delegation as is feasible is encouraged. Making employees responsible for budgets, no matter how small, empowers them by giving them a sense of responsibility and business awareness.

- **Structures for learning**. Learning must be encouraged at every level in the organisation. One way of doing this is to set up a corporate learning centre, which is a learning resource centre based in the company (see Chapter 11). Here, employees can do self-instructional training at their own pace and at times to suit themselves. Programmes may be text-, audio-, video- or computer-based. This makes learning accessible to all. This gives employees the facility to learn themselves when they need to or want to. Another way is to set up an educational support scheme for employees who want to pursue qualifications in their own time. A mentoring scheme can be established to encourage senior managers to pass on their expertise to younger members of staff. A bottom-up approach to learning is better than a top-down approach. The training and development department should be decentralised and line managers made responsible for the learning needs of their own staff. Learning champions should be appointed throughout the organisation to encourage employees' involvement in learning activities. Knowledge is power and capturing knowledge and converting into intellectual property through patents and copyrights can be a valuable source of revenue for the business. Implicit knowledge is thus made explicit.

- **Make employees responsible for their own learning**. Self-development of employees is actively encouraged. Staff draw up their own personal development plans. They are in a better position than anyone else to identify their own training and development needs and suggest ways in which these needs may be met. They are also more committed to plans that they draw up themselves. Development needs can be met by a combination of on-the-job and off-the-job training approaches. These can then be discussed and agreed with their supervisors and managers.

- **Benchmarking**. Sometimes the best and most powerful insights come from looking outside the organisation to gain a new perspective. Enlightened managers know that even companies in completely different businesses can be excellent sources of ideas and catalysts for creative thinking. So, as part of the process of continuous improvement, the company should track the best practices elsewhere and adopt them as appropriate. Customers, suppliers and competitors may be sources of ideas. You need to scan the environment for political, social, economic and technological developments. This process will be helped by attending conferences, visiting other companies to view their processes and scanning relevant magazines and publications. Learning means at least keeping up with, and ideally doing better than, your best competitors.

- **Strategic alliances**. You don't learn in isolation. You learn when you engage purposefully with others. The new paradigm is co-operation rather than competition. It is a type of networking. Companies can come together to share knowledge, technology, or business know-how. They achieve synergy by combining the strengths and overcoming the weaknesses of the firms making up the strategic alliance. In the airline industry, strategic alliances are becoming increasingly popular. Major airlines are trying to reduce costs, improve operations, increase the number of seats filled on each flight and ward off competition.

- **Teamwork**. A learning organisation is built on teams. Teams are groups of employees working on a specific assignment who collaborate together in a planned and systematic way in order to achieve goals. Trust, openness and cohesiveness are key characteristics of effective teams. An organisation structure is made up of interlocking teams. Teams use a participative approach where conflict is openly acknowledged and resolved, assignments are carried out to deadlines and work practices are continually reviewed and improved. Effective problem-solving and decision-making is central to teams. The team concept needs the long-term backing and commitment of senior management. Team-building programmes are needed to get the teams up and running. Team building is a process, not an event. Some companies have a once-off team-building event and then wonder why the organisation's teams are not successful.

- **Reward systems**. Learning should be rewarded and linked to performance appraisal schemes. This is part of the motivation and reinforcement principle. The reward system should be built into the structure of the organisation. A very basic system is the suggestion scheme, where small payments are given to employees for useful ideas. Other reward systems might include promotion, bonus schemes, profit-sharing schemes and employee share option schemes. Other things being equal, only employees with the right qualifications should be considered for promotional positions. Learning should be a discussion topic during the selection process for jobs.

The Role of the Manager

The role of the manager in developing a learning organisation can be recalled by the mnemonic MICA, which stands for **M**odel (as in role model), **I**ntegrator of learning, **C**hampion and **A**ctive provider of learning opportunities. MICA is explained in the following diagram:

ROLE OF MANAGER

Let's look at each of these points in some detail:

- **Model**. The manager must walk the talk. The manager must be a role model for learning. To do this, the manager must explicitly demonstrate by action and behaviour that he or she is an enthusiastic learner and developer. For example, if there is a corporate learning centre in the organisation, the manager must support the centre by attending and doing courses. He or she must also encourage staff to do courses in the centre.

- **Integrator of learning**. The manager must integrate learning into all aspects of the business. Learning opportunities on the job must be provided to meet the training and development needs of staff. Managers should encourage their staff to engage in prospective learning and retrospective learning activities. Before the training course, managers should discuss the prospective learning to be gained by attending the programme. After staff attend training programmes, they should review the learning achieved with staff and how it can be applied to the work situation.

- **Champion for learning**. Managers should become learning champions, selling the advantages of learning to senior management, their colleagues and other members of staff.

- **Active provider**. Managers should actively provide learning opportunities for their staff. This would include designing on-the-job learning activities for staff. Managers should actively encourage their staff to take up these learning opportunities.

Learning Tips for Individuals

Employees are the building blocks of the organisation. Employees need to be taught learning to learn skills if the learning philosophy is to permeate the whole organisation. The following are some practical tips for employees who want to make a contribution to the learning organisation:

- Review after each learning event. All job activities are potential learning events. The review should be as quickly after the event as possible.

- All action learning events should have a deadline for completion. Deadlines focus the mind and prevent drift.

- Improve your learning skills by doing accelerated learning courses or reading books on the topic. There are also some very good tape-based programmes which can be purchased.

- Develop facilitation skills. As a manager, supervisor or team leader, you need to be a facilitator of learning. People need to be encouraged rather than directed to learn.

- Develop a personal development plan. Identify your learning needs, design a suitable learning programme and evaluate the effectiveness of the learning. Integrate on-the-job learning opportunities with formal training.

- Identify learning opportunities. This could on-the-job and off-the-job. They could be inside the organisation or outside. All job activities should be seen as potential learning opportunities.

- Share your learning experiences with others. We learn by doing and we learn from others. If you share your learning with others they are more likely to share their learning with you. So everybody benefits.

- Encourage access to learning. If you use the corporate learning centre, you might encourage others to use it as well. If you are pursuing part-time studies, you may encourage colleagues to do likewise.

- Reading is a great form of learning. Read widely around business issues. Set yourself the goal of reading a management book each week. Most people discontinue reading after their formal education. They thus lose a great opportunity to expand their mental horizons.

Triggers for the Learning Organisation

Sometimes a company becomes a learning organisation through necessity. A company's cost base is out of control and losses have been incurred. The company faces bankruptcy or closure unless something drastic is done. Drastic problems demand drastic solutions. This then acts as the catalyst to greater learning, innovation and change.

A new broom sweeps clean. A new chief executive is appointed with a change mandate. The chief executive believes in the need to make learning an integral part of the operations of the business. Japanese companies, for example, have a reputation for their commitment to learning because of its tangible impact on the business in the form of improved morale, increased efficiency and greater profitability.

The company adopts a new mission and strategic objectives. This might be dictated by changing business needs. The market has changed or the needs of customers have changed. A company should all the time be anticipating likely changes in the environment so that it is ready when the change happens. An opportunity in the market triggers off the need to learn new processes and procedures.

The company appoints a champion for learning. Learning sets are established throughout the company and learning is integrated into team-building exercises. Structures and reward systems are put in place to encourage learning.

Inhibitors to a Learning Organisation

These can operate at three levels: strategic, structural and cultural. At the strategic level, it might be that the company has failed to integrate learning into its strategic planning process. The training and development plans should be linked to business needs and ultimately to the strategic objectives of the company. Learning should pay for itself in the form of identified outcomes such as increased sales or improved productivity.

A command-and-control management style operates in the company. Learning thrives under a participative style of leadership and withers under a directive style. Learning is seen as a cost rather than an investment. Consequently, there is no training budget or the training budget is inadequate. Research has shown that the companies with the greatest investment in learning are the most successful. The company has a top-down approach to training and development rather than a bottom-up approach. This means that line managers see the training and development department as responsible for training rather than themselves.

The organisation has no tradition of learning. It just does not believe that learning *per se* is worthwhile. The company is task-focused rather than people-focused. The emphasis is on getting the job done rather than the learning and developmental needs of people. Knowledge is kept at the top and only managers are sent on training and development programmes. Training is only given to poor performers rather than seen as a natural part of company life. Mistakes are not seen as learning opportunities and the company operates management by blame. Managers are governed by the "not invented here syndrome" and so have no interest in anybody else's ideas.

Managers believe that considering how things have been done in the past is more important than thinking about how they should be done in the future. They don't inspire staff to do their best for the company. They don't provide the best environment for learning by regularly providing feedback of work performance to enable staff to learn from their mistakes and improve in the future.

Learning Models for Organisations

Single-loop and Double-loop Learning

Single-loop learning is where an organisation improves its ability to achieve known objectives. It is associated with routines and behavioural learning. In single-loop learning, an organisation learns without making any significant change to its basic assumptions. Single-loop learning is also known as adaptive learning. In recent years, General Motors, IBM and Sears have made many adaptive changes. However, they still experienced much difficulty with their basic assumptions, cultural values and organisation structure, because they did not go beyond mere adaptive learning.

Double-loop learning is a type of transformational learning, reframing or paradigm shift. Here, the company re-evaluates the nature of its objectives and the values and beliefs surrounding them. This type of learning involves changing the organisation's culture and redefining its mission. Importantly, double-loop consists of the organisation's learning how to learn. Double-loop learning is also known as generative learning. It involves creativity and innovation, going beyond just adapting to change to being ahead of, anticipating change. The generative process leads to a total reframing of an organisation's experiences and learning from that process. It may involve developing a new business, new products or new markets.

Reg Revans formulated a simple model: $L \geq C$. This means that learning must be at least equal to or greater than the rate of change if a company wishes to survive in the marketplace. If an organisation's rate of learning does not keep up with change, then the organisation will eventually die. These days, the environment changes quite rapidly. There are political, legal, economic, social, ecological and technological changes happening all the time. Keeping tabs on these changes by scanning the environment is an important way of learning. Some companies have intelligence units established to monitor all aspects of change.

Knowledge Conversion Model

This model was invented by Ikujiro Nonaka and Hirotaka Takeuchi. It highlights the importance of capturing knowledge and making it explicit so that it can be used elsewhere in the organisation or sold outside to others. The model is illustrated in the following diagram:

KNOWLEDGE CONVERSION MODEL

	Tacit Knowledge to	*Explicit Knowledge*
Tacit Knowledge	Socialisation	Externalisation
Explicit Knowledge	Internalisation	Combination

(rows labelled *from*)

- **Socialisation** is the process where tacit knowledge is passed from one person to another. Tacit knowledge is knowledge that is understood but not expressed in writing. For example, a craft apprentice learns by watching the master craftsman. Learning is through demonstration, observation, imitation and practice. The apprentice is socialised into the craft. However, socialisation is a rather limited form of knowledge creation. The knowledge is transferred to the apprentice without either the apprentice or the master gaining any systematic insight into their craft knowledge. The knowledge does not become explicit or captured in any tangible form and as a result the company is unable to use it elsewhere. Made explicit, the knowledge becomes intellectual property, which could be used to train other apprentices or generate revenue for the company.

- **Externalisation** is the process where tacit knowledge is made into explicit knowledge. This happens when the master craftsman is able to articulate his knowledge so that it can be recorded and used to train others without the craftsman being present. This opens up all sorts of possibilities for the company. For example, the knowledge might be made into a software programme. It has now become intellectual property that can be used by trainees or sold to external clients. Explicit or recorded information can be discussed, debated, and improved upon.

- **Internalisation** is where explicit knowledge is shared with others so that they make it part of their own store of knowledge. In other words, they have internalised the explicit knowledge and made it tacit. Internalisation supports true understanding.

- **Combination** is where explicit knowledge is integrated with more explicit knowledge. For example, a management accountant may combine knowledge from different parts of the company and put it in a new format to assist managers to make better decisions. All that has happened is that existing knowledge has been reinforced. This does not add to the organisation's total knowledge.

Summary

A learning organisation is one that values learning. A learning organisation believes learning should be fun, participation should be the norm, communication should be open and that the customer is king. The core beliefs of a learning organisation were listed.

Certain things must be done to achieve a learning organisation. These include:

- Policies of decentralisation and delegation must be adopted;

- Structures must be put in place to facilitate learning;

- Employees must be made responsible for their own learning;

- Strategic alliances should be entered into to benefit the company;

- Teamwork is the building block on which a learning organisation should be built;

- Reward systems should be put in place to encourage learning.

Individual employees and managers play a vital role in developing a learning organisation. The triggers and inhibitors to a learning organisation were discussed.

Some learning models were discussed, including single-loop and double-loop learning. Revans's $L \geq C$ model — learning should be equal to or greater than change — was touched on. A model highlighting the importance of making tacit knowledge explicit was discussed. Intellectual capital is created by making tacit knowledge into explicit knowledge.

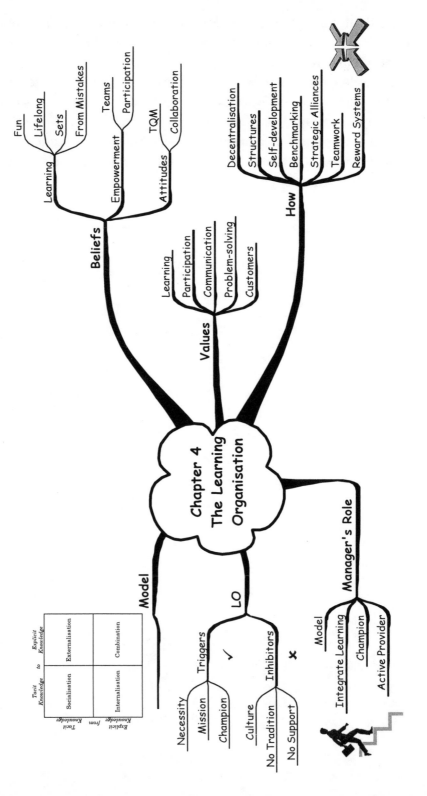

5

Learning Opportunities
and Resources

*"You grab a challenge, act on it, then honestly reflect on
why your actions worked or didn't. You learn from it
and then move on. That continuous process of lifelong
learning helps enormously in a rapidly changing
economic environment." — John Kotter*

 ◆ *What learning resources are available to me?*

 ◆ *What is the ASPIRE model of management development?*

 ◆ *What is the Performance Potential Model?*

 ◆ *What is the career life cycle?*

 ◆ *How does plateauing happen?*

 ◆ *How can I learn from change?*

 ◆ *Why are learning to learn skills so important?*

Support

To succeed in our careers, we need the support of employers, family, partners and friends. Many organisations now have educational support schemes, which actively encourage and financially support employees who desire to do third-level or postgraduate qualifications in their own time. Doing a third-level course part-time is a huge commitment on the part of employees and it is right that employers support such initiatives. In addition, organisations have training and development departments that support internal and external training programmes. They may also have mentors to advise and support employees in their career planning. You are blessed if you have a boss committed to staff development and who actively encourages you to achieve your goals.

Without the support of family, friends and partners, it would indeed be difficult to advance in your career. People who undertake self-development programmes have to be selfish with their time if they want to succeed. You need to designate huge chunks of your time to attending night classes or study. This time commitment needs to be negotiated with those around you who are affected. You need their understanding, encouragement and support so it is important that they are included in your plans. You are committed to a study programme so you won't be available on designated nights for social activities.

Learning Resources — Yourself

In your quest for self-development and career advancement, there are many techniques and resources available. These include:

- **Biography work**. This looks at the whole of your life. It records the movement of your life in the past and allows you to project to a future desired state. It gives you an opportunity to reflect on where you have been in the past, where you have succeeded and where you have gone wrong, and where you plan to go in the future. What are the motives that drove you in the past, and what are the motives that will drive you in the future? You should be clear in your own mind why you want to succeed in your career. The motives are called career anchors or career drivers and may include income, power, achievement, recognition, security and so on.

- **Learning logs**. This is a diary for recording and reflecting on your learning experiences. An unconsidered life is not worth living and certainly is not very productive from a learning point of view. The learning log encourages you to apply the learning cycle of do, reflect, conclude and do something differently. Many successful people in history kept diaries and journals, including da Vinci, Darwin, Faraday and Newton. The surviving 5,000 pages of Leonardo's notebooks contain research into anatomy, mechanics, hydraulics, and a wide range of other sciences. The notebooks also detail many civil and engineering schemes, plus designs for numerous mechanical devices, including a bicycle and a helicopter. Although never made in his lifetime, they do show how accurate a vision of the future he had and what a meticulous note-taker he was. Why not model yourself on the great figures of history and keep a learning log?

- **Libraries**. These are an amazing source of information and are inexpensive and often free. Libraries can be public, professional or corporate. Public libraries offer a wide range of information, while professional libraries are usually specialised. Some large companies have their own in-company library in addition to corporate learning centres. After their formal education, most people do not read non-fiction books. Why not start by setting yourself the goal of reading one management book a month and building from there?

- **Diagnostic instruments**. These are devices for self-analysis and self-awareness. They are usually in the form of questionnaires which you complete to find out your strengths and weaknesses in a particular area. From a manager's perspective, they are useful feedback devices that can help a manager learn more effectively. Make sure the instruments you use are from a reliable source and have been validated. Some diagnostic instruments may need the guidance of an occupational psychologist. The Honey and Mumford Learning Styles Questionnaire will determine your dominant learning styles. The styles are activist, reflector, theorist and pragmatist (see Chapter 2). Psychometric tests are taken to determine attitudes or abilities in specific areas. They are based on the assumption that certain qualities such as personality, attitudes, skills, abilities, competencies, preferences and values can be measured with reasonable scientific accuracy. They are often used to determine people's suitability for certain jobs. The Myers-Briggs Type Indicator is a psychometric test that assesses four dimensions of personality. These are *extroversion* or *introversion*; *sensing* or *intuiting*; *thinking* or *feeling*; and *judging* or *perceiving*. The model helps you become aware of the type of person you are and what particular strengths you have to offer. There are several instruments available for diagnosing team roles (see Smither et al., 1996). These include Belbin's, the Margerison-McCann Team Management Index and the Strength Deployment Inventory. Although they are designed specifically for teams, they also provide important insights for personal development. The McBer Management Styles Questionnaire helps you become aware of your leadership style. The styles assessed are *coercive*, *authoritative*, *affiliative*, *democratic*, *pacesetting* and *coaching*. As well as getting feedback from your manager, you may also get feedback from your work colleagues. This is called 360-degree feedback. Some companies may include customers, suppliers and other stakeholders in the process.

- **Managerial models**. These provide conceptual frameworks to help you understand and grasp organisational situations better. Well-known models include Blake's Managerial Grid, the Product Life Cycle, the Growth Share Matrix, the Johari Window, Maslow's Hierarchy of Needs and so on.

- **Personal computers**. The PC enhances your brainpower. Word-processing, spreadsheets, databases and graphics packages all increase your personal efficiency and productivity. Through the Internet, you have access to a vast resource of knowledge and learning. With e-mail, you have instant networks to make contact for business or self-development. There is now a vast range of CD-ROMs available on practically every subject under the sun, and reasonably priced too! The PC can become your personal tutor and learning centre.

- **Personal library**. As a committed self-developer, you should build up your own personal library. Books, specialist magazines, audiotapes, videos and CD-ROMs can be built up into a comprehensive self-development resource. You should build up a scrapbook of articles cut from newspapers on self-development topics. Relevant radio and TV documentaries may also be a source of self-development.

- **Personal development plan**. This is a plan that identifies your personal strengths and weaknesses, identifies training and development needs and specifies goals for your self-development. Personal development plans promote self-responsibility and a sense of ownership for personal, educational and career development. It may be the output from an assessment centre, a workshop or a performance appraisal scheme. Ideally, personal development plans should be linked to annual business plans and strategic plans. Once formulated, they should be implemented and followed through to completion. They should be updated each year or even more frequently. You should draw up your own personal development plan, even if the company in which you work does not support the process.

Learning Resources — Groups

- **Learning sets**. Learning sets can be a vital ingredient in a self-development programme. Each person in the learning set will keep a learning log in which they review their learning experiences. The members of the learning set will facilitate the process. We need colleagues to support, challenge and improve our learning and problem-solving skills. The central task of the learning set is to successfully complete the task that they have taken on. The learning set will need a facilitator so that everyone gets an opportunity to air his or her views and receive feedback. Because of the time factor, it is suggested that six members is a good number for a set. It is through feedback and reflection that we learn. The learning set is based on a number of principles, such as the fact that we learn best when supported and challenged by others, and that it is easier to accept feedback from peers rather than superiors.

- **Networking**. Networking is about contacting other people inside or outside the organisation. Contacts can help you do work faster and achieve your career goals quicker. In the business context, it is usually about information exchange. Both parties to the exchange benefit. Some experts believe that the hierarchical structure has outlived its usefulness and that networking is the way forward. Networking can get products to markets quicker, provide better customer service and help liaise more effectively with suppliers, customers and stakeholders.

- **Team learning**. People learn more effectively in groups because of the sharing of knowledge, support and feedback. Modern organisations are now built on the team concept.

- **Professional bodies**. Organisations such as the Institute of Personnel and Development specialise in personal and organisational development. They produce a huge range of books on self-development and training and these would be worth including in your self-development programme.

- **Mentors**. Mentors are people who can advise, support and counsel you in your career aspirations. Mentors can be part of your personal as well as your business life. Many successful business people attribute their success to having being mentored at an early stage in their careers.

- **Training and development specialists**. This is a resource within your own organisation that few people in practice avail of as much as they should. These are the specialists in all aspects of learning and development and their expertise should be called upon as you need it. They are often only too willing to help you in your quest for self-development.

The ASPIRE Self-Development Model

ASPIRE is a mnemonic which stands for **A**ssess, **S**WOT, **P**lan, **Im**plement, **R**eview and **E**valuate. It is a systematic process of self-development. The ASPIRE model is illustrated in the following diagram:

ASPIRE MODEL

Let's now examine each of these steps in more detail:

Assess your current position

Decide where you are now. Decide your future desired state — where you want to be. Consider how you can get there. Successful learners think about missions, roles, values, visions and goals. A mission is discovering the purpose of your life. A role is the various identities you have to assume to achieve your mission. Values are what is important to you. Vision translates your life purpose into images specific enough to inspire. Without a vision, you don't know where you are going and without assessing your current position you don't know where you are starting from.

The conflict between the vision and the reality of your present position drives you forward. Your subconscious generates the energy to achieve the vision. Goals are the specific results you want to achieve to fulfil your mission. Once you set a goal, the reticular activating system in the brain heightens your awareness to new information, which will help you achieve your goal. For examples, this is why when you decide to do research on a particular topic, you suddenly begin to identify sources of information and ideas for your topic all around you. You have programmed your mind to meet your need for relevant information.

The goals should be consistent with your values. There is a big difference between having a dream and becoming a successful learner. Not all dreamers achieve but all achievers are dreamers. Remember Martin Luther King's famous speech: "I have a dream"? Successful learners support their dreams with action plans. Success comes to those people who dream things and then take the necessary practical actions to make their dreams come true.

In summary, ask yourself:

- Where am I now?

- Where do I want to be?

- How can I get there? What is preventing me from getting there? Are my values and behaviours in harmony with my purpose? Are the goals of the organisation in which I work in harmony with my personal development goals?

- How will I know when I arrive? What income, house, car and lifestyle will I have?

- What kind of person do I want to be? Material possessions are not the only indicators of success. Looking after your spiritual needs is also important.

- What do I want to do with my life?

- What would I do if I knew I couldn't fail?

- What is holding me back? Money, time, knowledge, experience, skills or support?

Swot

SWOT stands for *strengths, weaknesses, opportunities* and *threats*. Strengths might include your positive attitude, experience, qualifications, and good IQ. Weaknesses might include a lack of certain skills, your tendency to harbour negative thoughts, be reactive and to procrastinate. An opportunity might be an offer of promotion while a threat might be the possibility of company closure and redundancy.

Carry out a strengths and weaknesses analysis of your capabilities. Try to turn weaknesses into strengths and threats into opportunities. Redundancy has often been turned into an opportunity where people have become successfully self-employed, releasing talents that they never knew they possessed.

Do a skills self-assessment. This concentrates on the skills we have in relation to the skills we need to do our job more effectively or progress in our careers. Examples include information technology, presentation, negotiation and assertiveness skills. There are ready-made checklists that can help with your self-assessment. Those for technical skills tend to be specific while those for mental and behavioural skills tend to be more general. We can focus on those areas where our current level of expertise falls below our desired level. Notice the gap between your existing level of experience and knowledge and the desired level. Consider what you need to do to fill it. This might include further experience, training and educational qualifications. Write down your long-term and short-term targets.

Plan

Draw up an action plan to achieve your long-term and short-term goals. This needs to be as specific as possible, with time and other resources clearly set out. You are primarily responsible for your own development. If you don't make it happen, nobody else will. In the long term you may need to do an MBA or professional qualification to give you the competitive edge and help you get ahead in the future. These long-term projects require a huge commitment of time and resources on your part. Generally, the more you learn the more you'll earn.

In the short term, you will need to continually update your knowledge, skills and experience. You can achieve this through attending continuing professional education courses run by your professional institute and by a planned programme of reading business books. You may need to develop all-round computer expertise such as word-processing, database management, spreadsheet, graphical presentation skills, e-mail and the Internet. Consider the resources you will need to acquire to support and be successful in your plan. Resources include finance, equipment, knowledge, skills and help from others.

It is important that you take responsibility for your goals and that they are an integral part of your action plan. Goals keep you focused, mobilise your energies and give you a sense of purpose. To set goals:

- Write them down. Some authorities claim that goals written down are over 20 times more likely to be achieved than goals not made explicit.

- See yourself achieving the goals. Specify the situation in which it will be achieved.

- Feel and experience the evidence that will tell you that your goals have been achieved.

- Put a time limit on them. Time limits concentrate the mind.

- Clarify why you want to achieve them.

- Commit yourself to definite targets.

- Share them with colleagues. This will act as an incentive to persevere in order not to lose face.

Setting goals is only half the battle. Pursuing them tenaciously and effectively is the other half. Many people fail to reach their potential in life because of a lack of realistic goals.

Implement

Decide the *steps* to be taken and the *deadlines* that will make things happen realistically. Reduce it to manageable (daily/weekly) steps. Focus your concentration by doing one thing at a time. Edison, probably the most prolific and greatest inventor of modern times, always concentrated on one thing at a time.

Write daily "to do" actions into your diary. Tick them off as you achieve them. This will concentrate your mind, give you a sense of purpose, accomplishment and satisfaction and help motivate you to continue.

Review

Write down the rewards (immediate, intermediate and final) to yourself when you have achieved your goals and sub-goals. Compare your actual performance and achievements against your goals. Vividly imagine your successes. What will you feel, hear, see and do on the achievement of your goals? What praise, compliments, recognition and respect will you earn? See yourself graduating with that MBA! Imagine the scene and sense of elation. Feel the pride of the occasion. A combination of desire, imagination and expectancy will keep you going and see you through in the end.

Evaluate

How successful have you been in achieving your personal development goals? What can you learn from your setbacks or mistakes? What corrective action do you need to take to put things right and get you back on target again? Evaluation is an ongoing process of continuous improvement against sub-goals until your desired end-goal is achieved.

The Performance Potential Model

Management succession is an important part of human resource planning. Organisations need to have a plan in place to fill management positions that may arise in the future due to retirements, resignations, deaths and expansions. The performance potential model will help you see how you stand in the management succession stakes. This model will help you categorise yourself as regards potential for promotion or otherwise. It views managers as rising stars, core managers, question marks and deadwood. To progress in your career, you need to be perceived as a rising star. In practice, you may have to get a trusted colleague to place you in a quadrant of the model, as you are unlikely to be honest and objective about your own potential or lack of potential. In any event it will be interesting to see how you are perceived by others. This will be useful as a feedback mechanism and as a benchmark for comparison with your own perceptions about yourself. You can then take corrective action to put your career back on target again. The Performance Potential Model is illustrated in the following figure:

PERFORMANCE POTENTIAL MODEL

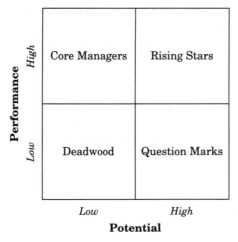

Source: Armstrong (1993)

- **Rising stars** are managers with the potential to go further. They have high potential and high performance. These managers will benefit from career planning, wider experience and management training. The company may wish to fast-track them by rapid promotion, challenging experiences and training and development opportunities. You should realise that getting into senior management positions takes hard work, ambition, loyalty and dedication, competing with others, and many years of experience. Only the best get through to senior management positions. Your chances are enhanced if you have a primary degree in some aspect of business, a professional qualification, or better still an MBA. You can determine to a large extent the direction of your career by getting the right experience, networking with the right people, taking on responsibility at an early age and qualifying in the right disciplines. You will also need to become visible to top management before the age of 30. Accountancy, marketing and engineering are some of the most popular disciplines for those at the top. You will also need to develop interpersonal relationship skills, negotiation skills, broad business skills, leadership skills, the ability to achieve results and the willingness to take risks. Take responsibility to positively influence the direction of your career.

- **Core managers** are those that the organisation depends on to
get things done. They have high performance but low potential.
They are the backbone of the organisation and provide stability
and continuity. They are good at doing their existing jobs but
are considered not to have the potential for further promotion.
They do not meet the criteria set by the organisation for senior
management positions. Nevertheless, they need training to keep
their morale high and expertise up-to-date. It is important to
have incentives in place to keep these managers interested and
motivated and they should not be taken for granted. The important role they play in the organisation should be acknowledged
explicitly. If you are ambitious and have your eyes set on the top
management positions, you don't want to be categorised as a
core manager. These managers have plateaued. These managers often lack flair, creativity and a willingness to take risks.
They are often set in their ways and are unlikely to be lifelong
learners. To succeed in management, you need a willingness to
take risks, a desire to seek new opportunities and a capacity to
generate more sound ideas than your colleagues.

- **Question marks** are those managers who, for whatever reason, do not seem to be making the grade. They have high potential but low performance. They may have the ability but lack the
motivation or they may have the motivation but lack the ability.
In any event, something should be done about them. Those with
the motivation but lacking skills may be brought up to standard
by further on-the-job and off-the-job training. Those with the
ability but lacking motivation should be encouraged by an appropriate incentive scheme. Here again, it is not in your future
interest to be classified as a question mark. You don't want to
be written off early in your career. Sometimes if you give a dog a
bad name it sticks with them for the rest of their careers. You
should be curious, enthusiastic and interested in your job. These
are often the qualities that get you noticed and recommended
for promotional positions. You must realise that learning is a
lifelong, self-directed activity and that you can influence the direction of your career. You should be anticipating the skills that

you may require for future roles and taking action to acquire
them.

- **Deadwood** are managers who have reached the level of their
  incompetence and are coasting towards retirement. They have
  low potential and low performance. They are the type of manager who have literally retired on the job. They are not good for
  the company and are blocking rising stars from potential promotional positions. They often have a chip on their shoulders
  because of perceived wrongs done to them in the past. They may
  feel that they have been unfairly treated in the promotion
  stakes. Their negative attitudes may be transmitted to younger
  managers, which is something you don't want to happen. Early
  retirement might be the solution for those who want to pursue
  other interests. From your own point of view, you don't ever
  want to be classified as a deadwood manager. If your career has
  come to a stop, you should calmly and objectively analyse the
  reasons why. You may have to consult a trusted colleague to get
  a true objective view. You are too close to the problem to be objective about it yourself. A change of company might solve your
  problem, if you feel you are going nowhere in your existing job.
  Early retirement might be a solution if you feel you have marketable skills which could be successfully used by other employers or in a self-employed capacity.

Career Stages

People have a life cycle: birth, growth, maturity and decline.
Similarly, people's careers go through different physical and psychological stages. Successful development consists of matching opportunities with the appropriate stage in your management career.
Schein has developed one of the most successful models of career
development. Because changes between stages is gradual and people enter stages at different ages, several of Schein's stages overlap.
The model of career development is shown below:

CAREER STAGES

- **Growth, fantasy and exploration (ages 0–21).** In the later parts of this stage, a person collects information about possible careers and is exploring options.

- **Entry into the world of work (ages 16–25).** Here a person learns how to seek out, apply for and be interviewed for a job. Acquiring CV writing, interview technique and selling skills is a priority.

- **Basic training (16–25).** Here a person gets acclimatised to the work and adjusts themselves to the culture of the organisation. This includes induction training.

- **Full membership in early career (ages 17–35).** The person develops job competencies and decides whether their personal goals are in harmony with the organisation. At age 25+, some people make a decision on whether they want to specialise in a particular area or move into general management.

- **Mid-career crisis (ages 35–45).** Here the person reassesses their progress in relation to their ambitions. Managers in this stage decide between reducing their efforts, changing their careers, or moving on to new challenges. Another important issue here is how to balance career demands with the demands of family life and recreational needs.

- **Late career in non-leadership role (age 40 to retirement).**
  This is characterised by mentoring younger promising staff, becoming more specialised and accepting reduced influence and
  power, while at the same time seeking greater satisfaction outside of work.

- **Late career in leadership role.** This is an alternative to the
  previous role. Here the manager renews focus on the long-term
  interests of the organisation, selecting and developing staff and
  learning how to influence others.

- **Decline and disengagement (age 40 until retirement).**
  Here the manager learns to accept reduced levels of power and
  responsibility. This may be accompanied by declining motivation and competence. The manager needs to learn how to lead a
  life that is not dominated by work issues and develop interests
  outside of work.

- **Retirement.** The last stage of the career cycle requires adjust-
  ing to dramatic changes in lifestyle, role and standard of living.
  Depending on your attitude, retirement may provide a new
  lease of life to develop a new career.

Plateauing

Plateauing occurs when managers reach positions that no longer
offer a challenge and where there are no more promotional outlets
in the organisation. Plateauing has become more common in recent
years because of restructuring, downsizing and the move towards
flatter organisational structures. Because of the greater span of
control in flatter organisations, fewer managers are required.

Plateaus can be classified under three types:

- **Structural plateaus** happen because there are no more promotional outlets in the organisation. This may be due to delayering or downsizing. To overcome this problem, managers
  must either leave the organisation or develop a new specialisation to develop their careers.

- **Content plateaus** occur where managers have so much experience in their existing jobs that it no longer offers a challenge.

Content plateaus can be overcome by job rotation, jc
ment and job enrichment. Secondment and oversea
ments are other possibilities.

- **Life plateaus**. When managers have made their careers the
focus of their lives, an event such as being made redundant or a
personal crisis may cause them to reassess their careers and result in a serious psychological crisis. The meaning or purpose of
their life may be questioned and reinterpreted.

Benchmarking

Benchmarking is a great way of learning from the best practices of
others. Ideas should be creatively adapted to your own requirements, rather than mere imitation. Benchmarking should be a process, rather than a once-off effort at improvement. We can learn
from:

- **Customers**. Feedback from customers about service and quality of products is very useful. A questionnaire might be used to
gather this information. You may also benchmark the best practices in customer companies.

- **Competitors**. In the late 1970s, the Xerox Corporation realised
that Japanese competitors were selling copiers at prices that
Xerox could not match. Xerox set out to understand why and to
learn, from their competitors, concepts such as value engineering. Xerox also began to learn from competitors about other best
practice techniques.

- **Suppliers**. Companies should benchmark *activities*, not other
companies, and may reap the most benefits where the organisation is different to themselves. This is more likely to lead to
creative adaptation of ideas.

- **Other parts of your own organisation**. Companies can
benchmark their own best practice as well as that of others, and
increasingly do so in the "soft" areas of human resource management through the use of employee attitude surveys.

- **Peers**. Take on board the best practices and behaviour of colleagues at work while ignoring the worst parts.

- **Modelling through Neuro-Linguistic Programming**. Study the way successful managers you admire do certain things and copy their actions. Anti-role models can also be a source of modelling, provided you do the opposite of what they do. Learning from others' mistakes or inappropriate behaviour may mean you are learning how not to do something.

- **Improving your excellence through continuous improvement and learning**. Through observation, experimentation and continuous feedback, you can improve your performance as you go along. You will need standards of excellence and learning objectives for comparison purposes.

Learning from Change — Personal

Without change, there would be no need to learn. We learn by adapting successfully to change. Changes are opportunities waiting to be exploited. The following changes impact on managers personally:

- **Information technology**. Everybody is affected by information technology. It includes the personal computer, e-mail, the Internet, fax and so on. Managers can't afford to let information technology pass them by. You need to develop practical skills and keep up-to-date in this area if you want to survive and progress in your career. Some experts believe that the Internet is the greatest invention since the printing press.

- **Telework**. With modern technology, there is no need for people to commute in and out of work any more. You can substitute telecommunications for physical commuting. With information technology and telephone links, you can now work from home. Teleworkers make use of a range of equipment and services to perform their work, including personal computers with modems, telephones, Internet, e-mail, mobile phones, voice mail, fax machines and audio/video conferencing. Not all work is suitable for teleworking. Work that requires little face-to-face contact, high

concentration and that can be done to a deadline with little su-
pervision is particularly suitable. Consequently, teleworking is
popular with companies in research, software development, financial services, journalism and publishing. As technologies
improve and become more affordable, more organisations and
individuals are likely to adopt telecommuting as a new form of
work arrangement. There are downsides to both the employer
and the teleworker. The employer has concerns about start-up
costs and running costs, data security, loss of management control and the loss of face-to-face communication. The teleworker
may feel isolated and that their careers may be disadvantaged.

- **Part-time contracts**. This approach suits many people who
have family and other commitments. They may contract to work
half time so that they have spare time for other interests and to
develop other talents.

- **Self-employed**. Many senior managers are now retiring early
and taking up careers as self-employed management consultants. There are many advantages to being self-employed, including freedom from bureaucratic control and taxation
benefits.

- **Portfolio concept**. This is the concept of selling your services
to several employers instead of one. It also means developing a
range of skills so that you are more employable. It is a means of
spreading risk. Instead of putting all your eggs in the one basket, you spread them over many.

- **Adaptability**. There are no jobs for life anymore. However, you
may have many jobs in a lifetime. There is no security, just opportunity in the job market. You should aim for lifelong employability with many organisations rather than lifelong
employment with one organisation. Your investment in learning
will determine your future income.

Learning from Change — Organisational

The following changes are happening in organisations:

- **Restructuring**. Various terms such as reorganisation, reengineering, resizing, downsizing and delayering have been used to describe this process. The terms are often used interchangeably, but technically they do not mean exactly the same thing. In any event, the aim is usually to make an organisation more efficient, productive and effective. It can be applied to one or all the functions in a business such as finance, marketing, information technology, operations and human resource management. It may include removing management layers from the organisation; reducing the number of employees; redesigning work processes; and outsourcing work previously done by the company. As a manager, you should develop a wide range of marketable skills to increase your employability.

- **Autonomous work groups**. Sometimes called self-regulating and self-managing work groups. These are empowered groups of workers with a variety of skills who perform a discrete task. The group is given decision-making power to support its direct area of responsibility. It may be part of a human resource strategy to create labour flexibility and commitment. Generally, it has been found to increase motivation and job satisfaction. Employers in the future will be looking for employees who are self-starters and can accept responsibility.

- **Multiskilling**. Multiskilling develops a broad, highly skilled workforce. Organisations prefer a flexible workforce who are able to do a range of tasks across traditional demarcation lines. Multiskilling is a core aspect of empowered teams, increasing their versatility and flexibility. In large organisations with strong unions, it is often seen by skilled craftsmen as undermining their traditional skills.

- **Outsourcing**. This is often part of restructuring. It may involve closing down or selling off parts of the business and subcontracting the work to outsiders in the belief that it can be done more efficiently elsewhere; for example, in-house printing and canteen facilities.

- **Short-term contracts**. Many companies are now subcontracting work to new or former employees. From the company's perspective, this offers flexibility and less cost in the form of pension and other entitlements. From the contractee's perspective, it offers self-responsibility and some tax advantages as a self-employed person. With companies now actively outsourcing many of their former business activities, short-term contracts are a trend likely to increase in the future.

Learning to Learn

Peter Drucker maintains that the acquisition of "learning to learn" skills is vital for the future. The globalisation of markets, competition and information technology are some of the rapid changes taking place. Knowledge quickly becomes out-of-date and needs to be updated constantly if we want to survive in the modern business environment. Transformational learning is needed to take advantage of new opportunities and to anticipate future changes. Your education and professional training, in themselves, will no longer equip you for life. Many people on qualifying throw away their books, not realising that learning is a lifelong process. They should keep their books as a core library and supplement them as new ideas and developments arise. The need for lifelong learning has been recognised by the professions with their continuing professional education programmes.

Learning from Mistakes

In line with the concept of total quality management, doing it right first time should be our goal. Nevertheless, it is part of the human condition that mistakes will happen. Learned helplessness is where a person makes several mistakes while doing a particular task and then decides that the task is beyond them. They stop trying. This is tantamount to saying that you can't learn from your mistakes. Take responsibility for your mistakes and don't start blaming yourself or others. Blame discourages objective examination of the mistake and the circumstances surrounding it. We must learn from our mistakes so that they will not happen again. One approach might be to reflect on your mistakes by carrying out a cause-and-effect analysis:

- What kind or type of mistake took place?

- What is the effect of the mistake? What are its consequences, results and outcomes?

- What was the cause of the mistake? Knowing the cause of a mistake is essential before you can take the proper steps to correct it.

- How can I correct my mistake? How can I prevent the mistake from happening again? Observation and experiment will tell you what works and what does not work. You must take the appropriate corrective action.

The history of invention and discovery is a history of learning from mistakes, transformational learning, continuous learning and improvement. The road to creativity is strewn with errors which where not ignored but were objectively studied and analysed for the lessons to be learnt from them.

Christopher Columbus (1451–1506) discovered America by accident. On the morning of 12 October 1492, Christopher Columbus stepped ashore on an island known today as the Americas. He was seeking a western sea route from Europe to Asia. When he sighted land, he believed he had reached his goal. To the day he died he still believed that he had reached Asia. Although Columbus was mistaken, he still ranks as a great discoverer. Few other navigators of his time would have dared to sail westward into the unknown.

Summary

You need the support of your employer, family, friends and partners to advance in your career.

Learning resources include:

- Biography work
- Learning sets
- Learning logs
- Libraries
- Networking

- Team learning
- Diagnostic instruments
- Managerial models
- Personal computers
- Professional bodies
- Personal library
- Mentors
- Training and development specialists.

The ASPIRE self-development model stands for:

- **A**ssess your current position
- **S**WOT analysis
- **P**lan
- **I**mplement
- **R**eview
- **E**valuate.

The Performance Potential Model has four quadrants. *Core managers* have high performance but low potential. *Rising stars* have high performance and high potential. *Deadwood* has low performance and low potential. *Question marks* have low performance but high potential. Knowing how you rate in the model may help you influence the direction of your career.

Career stages, like the biological life cycle, go through a cycle of birth, growth, maturity and decline. Plateauing occurs when managers reach positions that no longer offer a challenge and where there are no further prospects of promotion.

Benchmarking is a method of learning from the best practices of others.

Without change, there would be no need to learn. We learn by adapting successfully to change.

Learning to learn is the vital skill for success in the future.

CHAPTER 5 LEARNING MAP

Chapter 5 Learning Opportunities and Resources

Resources
- Biography Work
- Learning
  - Sets
  - Logs
- Libraries
- Networking
- Teams
- Diagnostic Instruments
- PDP
- Mentors

ASPIRE
- Assess Current Position
- SWOT
- Plan
- Implement
- Review
- Evaluate

Potential
- Model

Benchmarking
- Customers
- Competitors
- Suppliers
- Peers

Career
- Stages
  - Start
  - Growth
  - Maturity
  - Decline
- Plateauing
  - Structural
  - Content
  - Life

Learning
- From Change
  - IT
  - Telework
  - Contracts
  - Self-employed
  - Porfolio
- Organisational
  - Restructuring
  - AWGs
  - Outsourcing
- To Learn

6

Accelerated Learning

*"To maximise your earning power,
maximise your learning power."* — *Anon*

- ◆ *How can I develop effective reading skills?*

- ◆ *How can I develop a powerful memory?*

- ◆ *Why should I use learning maps to improve my learning?*

- ◆ *How can I improve my concentration?*

- ◆ *Why is it important to be in the right state for learning?*

What is Accelerated Learning?

The conventional approach to learning assumed focused concentration and frequent repetition.

On the other hand, accelerated learning emphasises a relaxed state in a supportive environment, and engaging all the senses so that your left and right brains are involved. You can accelerate your learning by using the latest thinking in reading, memory, concentration and relaxation. Learning maps can be used to increase your all-round effectiveness as a learner.

Effective Reading

Reading is basic to learning and is one of the most important skills of everyday life. Reading opens up the door to a whole world of information. You can learn how to build or fix things, to enjoy novels, to discover how other people live, to exercise your imagination, to broaden your interests and to develop new ideas and concepts. Reading is the key to your intellectual development. By adopting the appropriate effective reading strategies, you can read faster, understand and learn more. Many of the great learners were great readers who were self-taught in their chosen discipline. Reading skills are a prerequisite to becoming a lifelong learner.

In the modern workplace, good reading skills are essential. Being able to read and comprehend manuals on how to operate systems, computers, and automated machinery is essential. In addition, being promoted often involves further study or attendance at training courses or workshops that call for advanced reading skills. If you are studying, use additional textbooks and study guides as resources. Each book will give you a different perspective on the subject and different examples. This is an excellent way to clarify difficult concepts and give you more practice at doing questions. You must read books and specialist magazines to keep up-to-date in your specialist field. Truly, a person's ability to read directly influences job and career success.

The average reader reads at about 240 words per minute. It is possible to read up to 800 words per minute with little comprehension loss. Psychologists have found that there is some comprehension loss above 400 words. They have also found that because of the ways our eyes function, there is a physical constraint of 800 words per minute for conventional reading. The following are some of the benefits of reading faster:

- It saves time.

- It is more efficient.

- You will broaden your mental horizons by reading more in less time.

- It will improve your understanding. People who read below 400 words per minute suffer a comprehension loss.

- It keeps you up-to-date.

- It is a mental challenge and tonic.

- It helps you study more effectively and pass exams.

- If you are writing a thesis, you can research more in less time.

There are five steps to being an effective reader:

1. **Establish a need**. Your job may involve a lot of reading and you want to learn how to do it more effectively. The need must be reinforced by a desire to improve your reading skills and a belief that it is possible.

2. **Understand the reading process**. You must understand how your eyes work and how to use this knowledge to improve your reading capacity.

3. **Understand why you read slowly**. This may be due to lack of confidence, word power or lack of technique. Reading tends to be slower when you are dealing with complex material or studying a subject for the first time. You may even need to reread portions of the text to understand it fully. On a second reading or when reviewing, reading speeds may be much faster.

4. **Learn new efficient reading habits** and get rid of the old.

5. **Practise the new reading skills**. Everything worthwhile takes time.

Poor readers may suffer from the following problems:

- They have small recognition spans. They read one word at a time.

- They make regressions, i.e. they re-read words or sentences which they feel they don't understand.

- They vocalise or sub-vocalise. In other words, they mouth the words or say them to themselves.

- They fail to vary their reading speed in line with their purpose.

- They fail to integrate their reading with experience and prior knowledge.

- They have a small working memory capacity.

The VERTIGO Model for Improved Reading

Reading involves certain skills such as word recognition, vocabulary development and comprehension. VERTIGO is a mnemonic which brings these skills together. It stands for **V**ocabulary, **E**yesight, **R**egression, **T**alking, **I**deas, **G**uide, and **O**perating reading speed. This mnemonic is illustrated in the following diagram. We will then discuss each of these points in detail.

IMPROVED READING — VERTIGO MODEL

Vocabulary
Eyesight
Regression
Talking
Ideas
Guide
Operating Reading Speed

- **Vocabulary**. A poor vocabulary is going to slow up your reading speed. This is especially so when you are reading a new subject for the first time. You are unfamiliar with much of the terminology and this slows up your reading and comprehension. It is a good idea to invest in a specialist dictionary to build up your vocabulary in the new subject. You should write down the definition of words that you do not know on cue cards and study them in your spare moments until they have gone into your long-term memory. Reading a good quality newspaper each day will also increase your word power. Study common prefixes and suffixes. A prefix is one or more syllables added at the start of a word to qualify its meaning, while a suffix is added at the end. For example, in the word "premeditated" the "pre", which means "before", is the prefix, meditate means to think, and the "ed" is the suffix, which refers to the past tense. In the word "photophobia", the prefix is "photo" which means light and "phobia" means fear. Photophobia means an abnormal sensitivity to light.

- **Eyesight**. If you have poor eyesight, then you need reading spectacles. It is surprising the number of people who need spectacles but don't get them due to vanity or inertia. Putting your eyes under pressure will cause headache and eye strain. During reading sessions, palm your eyes occasionally and focus your eyes alternately on a near and a distant object. This will relax and rest the eyes and prevent fatigue. Use your peripheral vision. Move in two words from the left. Finish two words from the right. Motorists are aware of peripheral vision when driving. Even though their eyes are focused straight ahead, nevertheless they are able to see the two extremes at the left and right and so they are aware of pedestrians about to come off the footpath.

- **Regression**. Regression may be due to habit, lack of concentration or poor vocabulary. Readers may also regress because they lose their place on the page. They begin reading something and realise that they've just read it a few moments before. Stop regressing. Don't go back over words you think you don't understand. More often than not, the meaning will become clear because of context and structure as you continue reading. In rare cases, regression may be necessary, as when reading complex legal or technical texts for the first time. Technical texts that tell us how to operate something usually require slow and thoughtful reading. You should also eliminate slow recovery time. Practise a smooth movement from one line to the next. Be ready to flip over to the next page.

- **Talking**. Moving your lips as if talking to yourself slows up your reading speed. Sub-vocalising is saying the words in your head, which most people do. However, if you desist from sub-vocalising structure words such as "and", "but" and so on, you will speed up your reading considerably. Saying words out loud can be very useful if you are revising study material, say for an examination. This is so because you are engaging both your auditory and visual senses. But for study reading other than revision, it is not recommended.

- **Ideas**. Read for ideas by grouping words together. The normal recognition span is two to three words. Practise using the editorial column in your daily newspaper to do this. Concentrate on the central area while letting your peripheral vision pick up the two extremes. Good readers are more concerned with comprehension and the meaning of the text rather than surface characteristics. Good comprehension involves selecting and understanding what you need; retaining and recalling that information; and connecting new information to existing knowledge and experience. Comprehension involves chunking individual words to get the idea at sentence level. The main idea or gist is worked out at paragraph level. Beyond the paragraph level, themes, which are often not stated explicitly, are inferred. Understanding themes goes beyond the main idea. Read with a purpose. Why are you reading? If you are researching a particular topic, then you concentrate on subject matter related to that topic. You need to be disciplined and ignore the rest. The index will direct you to areas of interest.

- **Guide**. Use a pencil as a visual guide. Run the pencil underneath the line as you go along. Vary the speed of your reading in line with your purpose and the familiarity of the text. The advantages of using a visual guide is that it improves concentration, prevents regression, reduces sub-vocalisation, increases perceptual span and creates rhythm. Reading is a left-brain process, while building up a rhythm engages the right brain.

- **Operating speed**. Count the number of words in a piece of text — say 500. Now time yourself reading this piece of text — say two minutes. Divide the 500 words by two minutes to get your operating speed per minute. In this case, it is 250 words per minute. You know that the average operating speed per minute is 240 words, so you should be happy that you are slightly better than average. However, it is possible to read up to twice this speed without any loss of comprehension. This then should be your goal: to bring up your speed to between 400 and 500 words per minute. Benchmark against your own performance rather than anybody else's. On the other hand, if your operating speed is below average, you should be concerned that you are not reading as fast or effectively as you should. You should practise the ideas presented in this section to bring you up to an acceptable speed. If you are studying for an examination, it might be a good idea to invest in a reading stand on which you can put your book. Place this about 15 to 24 inches away from you and use your pencil as a guide when reading. I would only do this for serious reading. Leisure time reading is for enjoyment and the words often need to be savoured and enjoyed. Be a flexible reader. Vary your reading speed in line with the difficulty or familiarity of the subject. Speed up when you come to text that you know and slow down with text that is new to you or is complex. Occasionally, you may decide to skip text that is very familiar to you.

The 3Ss of Speed-reading

- **Skimming**. This is done to get the gist of the topic. It is not conventional reading as we understand it. Skimming involves reading chapter headings, section headings, subheadings, topic sentences and chapter summaries. The objective is to get a quick overview of the topic. Make one-word summaries of each paragraph, combine these in the form of a learning map for each chapter and condense these into a learning map for the whole book. You now have a quick overview of the book, which you can review as the need arises.

- **Scanning**. This means looking through a book to quickly locate material relevant to your needs. Use the index at the back of the book as a guide to the particular location or locations of the book that interest you. When you find the desired information, you will read it carefully in line with your purpose. When researching a thesis, use this approach.

- **Skipping**. This means you skip information that you are familiar with or which is not in line with your purpose. There is no point in reading material that you already know. Concentrate on what is new or what specifically meets your current needs. When reading a novel, you do not have to read every word or sentence carefully to get the gist of the story.

SQ3R Method

This is a systematic approach to reading a textbook. It is used in many third-level colleges throughout the world. It is not a speed-reading method but rather a method to improve the effectiveness of your reading. It will improve your comprehension and recall of written material. It stands for **S**urvey, **Q**uestion, **R**ead, **R**ecall and **R**eview. This is illustrated in the following diagram:

THE SQ3R SYSTEM

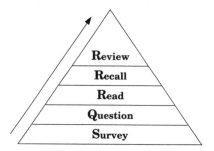

Let's now consider each of these in some detail:

- **Survey**. The purpose of the survey stage is to give you a quick overview of the contents of the book. Study the title page, preface, contents, index and leaf through the book quickly. Now that you have surveyed the book, adopt the same approach to each chapter. When surveying a chapter, pay special attention to the chapter title, section headings, subheadings, first and last paragraphs, topic sentence and the chapter summary, if provided. The first sentence in a paragraph is usually the topic sentence.

- **Question**. Now raise issues or questions that you want the book to address. Use a questioning approaching, asking what, why, when, how, where and who. This creates a void in your mind, which you will aim to fill. Reading with a purpose will focus your concentration on the issues that you need to know.

- **Read**. Reading is the third step, not the first. You will read the chapter twice. The first reading will be fast, to get the overall gist of the chapter. The second reading is slow and deliberate. It is during the second reading that I suggest you prepare a learning map, which will act as your permanent record and overview of the content of the chapter.

- **Recall**. Recall during the second reading. You should recall after each section and put your recall keywords on a learning map. Then check the section quickly again to make sure you have picked out the key ideas and filled in any gaps.

- **Review**. Review from your learning maps Operate to a review plan to counteract forgetting. For exam purposes, you will need to get the material from your short-term memory into your long-term memory. This is achieved by frequent review.

Increased Reading Powers of Observation

There are a few little tricks of the trade which you can use to improve your powers of observation when reading. Authors usually use visual and verbal signposts to highlight important ideas in the text. Visual signposts make words stand out to highlight their importance. They take the form of:

- Words in italic
- Words underlined
- Words in bold face
- Different type face
- Numbering of points
- Lettering of points
- Bullet points.

Visual signposts may also summarise key points visually in order to make them more digestible and understandable to the reader. They could take the form of any of the following:

- Tables
- Graphs
- Pictures
- Maps
- Diagrams
- Charts
- Models
- Learning maps.

Many readers are tempted to skip over these, as they interfere with the continuity of reading. However, this is a foolish approach as often they contain the kernel of the idea that the author is trying to get across. Also, in examinations, you can earn extra marks by being able to illustrate your answer visually.

Verbal signposts are words which authors use to compare, contrast, conclude or add to ideas. Examples include:

- *Firstly, secondly, etc.* means the author is about to list down the case supporting some argument.

- *On the other hand* means the author is about to give an exception or alternative viewpoint.

- *However* means the author is about to introduce a qualification.

- *For instance* means the author is about to give an example.

- *Furthermore* means the author is about to add ideas supporting the case.

- *Therefore* means the author is about to arrive at a conclusion.

- *Again* means the author is about to emphasise a point.

- *So* means the author is about to conclude or reinforce.

The Four Rs of Forgetting

1. **Retrieval failure** is where you cannot recall information from your memory when you need to. This is also known as the "tip of the tongue" experience. Sometimes you meet an acquaintance on the street but for some reason you are unable to recall their name. Shortly afterwards, the name pops into your head effortlessly. Psychologists compare it to trying to find something you've lost in a cluttered room. The object is still there; you just can't locate it at the moment. Similarly, the information is not gone, but neither can it be recalled immediately.

2. **Repression**. Freud believed we forget many things because we unconsciously wish to do so. These may be unpleasant or painful experiences that we feel are best forgotten. This is also called motivated forgetting. For example, people who like to gamble remember the few times they won rather than the many times they lost.

3. **Refabrication** or confabulation involves the unconscious invention of false memories. To compensate for the poor memory of something that happened a long time ago, we tend to fill in the gap with invented details. Refabricated memories seem real and are almost impossible to distinguish from the truth.

4. **Recall interference**. There are two types of interference — proactive and retroactive. *Proactive interference* happens when previously learned information interferes with a person's ability to remember new material. A previously learned computer package may interfere with your progress in learning a new one. Previously learned keyboard strokes may not give the same results as the previous package. *Retroactive interference* occurs when the learning of new facts may interfere with the memory of something previously learned. When you learn a new piece of prose, it will hinder the recall of a piece you previously learned. The testimony of witnesses to a crime can be influenced and shaped by the type of questions put.

The MEMORISATION Model

Everybody would like to have a good memory. Most of us don't for the simple reason that we have never learned how to use it effectively. There are many ways that you can help your memory to work more effectively. However, you need to work at it if you want to succeed. MEMORISATION is a model to help you remember the key approaches you can adopt to develop a good memory. This mnemonic is explained in the following diagram:

THE MEMORISATION MODEL

Mnemonics
Expectation
Mind Maps
Organisation
Repetition
Imagination
Senses
Association
Techniques
Intensity
Overlearning
Novelty

Mnemonics

Mnemonics are devices that help you remember information. This text is peppered with mnemonics to help you remember key aspects of learning. MEMORISATION itself is a mnemonic to help you remember the key aspects of memory. Overlearn the mnemonics and you will have them for all time.

The following will help you make your mnemonics more memorable:

• Use positive, pleasant images. The brain has a tendency to block out unhappy ones.

• Exaggerate the size of important aspects that you want to remember.

- Use humour and slapstick to make the items more memorable. Rude or sexual themes are usually very hard to forget. Combine these with movement for extra impact.

- Vivid, colourful images have more impact than drab ones. Colour is an enhancer of learning.

- Use a multisensory approach. Your mnemonic images can contain sounds, smells, tastes, touch, movements and feelings as well as pictures.

- Invent mnemonics for a knowledge area such as management that you need to remember. Link the various mnemonics in the form of a story so that you can remember whole areas of a subject.

Mnemonics have been used throughout this book as a way of helping you learn and recall key points. A mnemonist is a person with a trained memory. Rhymes are also useful devices for remembering things. The rhyme "Thirty days hath September . . ." helps you remember the number of days in each month of the year. Why not use some of the devices these experts use? Some examples of mnemonics are:

- NO CASH helps you remember the chemical and other constituents of coal. This stands for **N**itrogen, **O**xygen, **C**arbon, **A**sh, **S**ulphur and **H**ydrogen.

- HOMES contains the first letter of all the great lakes of North America, standing for **H**uron, **O**ntario, **M**ichigan, **E**rie, and **S**uperior. You can remember the sequence from west to east by using the sentence "**S**ome **M**en **H**ate **E**ach **O**ther". This device is known as an acrostic. As you can see, it uses the first letter of each word in a sentence to represent a piece of information to be remembered. The acrostic is an extremely useful tool in learning and remembering. It is also one of the most simple.

- PEST is used for environmental analysis. This stands for **P**olitical, **E**conomic, **S**ocial and **T**echnological.

- PAIN is used for recalling the various investment appraisal methods. This stands for **P**ayback, **A**ccounting rate of return, **I**nternal rate of return and **N**et present value.

- PLOCS recalls the functions of management. This stands for **P**lanning, **L**eading, **O**rganising, **C**ontrolling and **S**taffing.

- AIDA stands for **A**ttention, **I**nterest, **D**esire and **A**ction and is an aspect of sales promotion.

- SMART may be used to help you remember the characteristics of good objectives. They should be **S**pecific, **M**easurable, **A**ttainable, **R**elevant and **T**imely.

- APES may help you remember the major controls in a business. This stands for **A**nnual plan control, **P**rofitability control, **E**fficiency control and **S**trategic control.

To remember the names of the planets in our solar system, in order of proximity to the sun, use the sentence "**M**y **V**ery **E**ducated **M**other **J**ust **S**howed **U**s **N**ine **P**lanets". This stands for Mercury, Venus, Earth, Mars, Jupiter, Saturn, Uranus, Neptune and Pluto. The colours of the rainbow can easily be remembered by "**R**ichard **O**f **Y**ork **G**ave **B**attle **I**n **V**ain". This stands for Red, Orange, Yellow, Green, Blue, Indigo and Violet. These are more examples of acrostics.

You probably came across the memory device for remembering that stalactites hang on the ceiling of caves ("c for ceiling" or "tights down") while stalagmites come from the cave floor up ("g for ground" or "mites up").

"Principle" and "principal" are two words that are often confused with each other. To remember them for all time, learn "princip**le** is a **rule** while princip**al** is a **pal**". If you have problems remembering how to spell "believe", just remember "never be**lie**ve a **lie**". To distinguish "stationery" from "stationary", just visualise a large **env**elope for station**e**ry.

Why not invent your own mnemonics for critical areas of your studies or work, or for vital information that you need to remember? Research shows that when people are given a short time to study a list, those using mnemonics learn two to three times better than those who use an unstructured approach.

Expectation

Attitude has much to do with whether you will remember something or not. If you think you can, you will. If you think you can't, you won't. You are more likely to remember something if you expect to remember it. Say to yourself, "I will remember everything I study today." However, if you believe that you have a bad memory, you will be proved right!

Mind Maps

These are also known as learning maps. This is a multidimensional note-taking device which will help you remember better and learn more effectively. It concentrates on key words and therefore avoids filling up your mind with clutter. The mind is more likely to recall key words rather than phrases and sentences. Learning maps are dealt with comprehensively later in this chapter.

Organisation

Organising things into relevant categories will help you remember them more effectively. Grouping things in logical ways makes them more meaningful for recall. Information that is organised can be learnt much faster than information that is not. Reading strategies that pay attention to individual ideas, and how they are organised and related, produce better recall. There are three techniques for mental organisation:

1. Sequencing or putting items into chronological or alphabetical order;

2. Categorising or grouping things according to some common characteristic such as colour, shape or other similarity;

3. Relational imagery or organising items around a theme such as work, holidays, Christmas and so on.

People remember things better in relation to a particular context. Contextual features become associated with material being learned, and can serve as cues for recall.

The recency and primacy effect suggests that we remember things better at the start of a list and at the end. In between, we are inclined to forget. You can use this phenomenon in making presentations by putting your important key ideas at the start and again at the end. In between, you can make things unique and outstanding to capture attention. The principle is captured in the saying: "Tell them what you're going to tell them, tell them and tell them what you've told them." This is a key aspect of presentation skills. The principle also suggests that the more starts and finishes in a study period, the better. Immediately after you have learnt something is the time when your memory for it is best. This is called the "reminiscence effect". Frequent breaks allow you to take advantage of this.

Repetition

The more frequently you repeat something, the more likely you are to recall it. Repetition strengthens the pathways in the brain. Overlearning ensures that the item goes from your short-term memory to long-term memory storage. Overlearn so that in the examination room you won't have difficulty recalling information, even if under stress.

The best way to commit a passage to memory is by the "progressive part method". In this method, the learner adds a new line while continuing to rehearse the other lines. For example, if you learn line one, you would then learn lines one and two. When you have these memorised you would then tackle lines one, two and three, and so on. Such procedure ensures:

- That our short-term memory is not overloaded;

- The practice and retention of earlier lines, otherwise forgotten through interference.

For best results, the "progressive part method" should be combined with the "holistic method". In other words, get an overview of the material first before using the progressive part method. This is the concept behind the SQ3R system. Build up a framework of the area to be studied and then develop this as your studies progress.

Imagination

Picture them in your mind's eye or form the key ideas into a story to remember them more effectively. Use the MUSE principle: **M**ovement, **U**nusualness, **S**lapstick and **E**xaggeration. The more ridiculous it is, the better.

Get a deep vivid impression of what you want to remember. To do this, you must concentrate and focus your attention on the material you are studying. Use your powers of observation. A camera won't take good pictures in poor lighting conditions. Similarly, your mind won't register and remember impressions when there are inconsistencies in your mental ideas of a subject.

Impression is therefore the ability to imagine or picture what you want to remember in your mind's eye. Reading is a left-brain function. This is the side of the brain that specialises in logic, words, numbers and language. To make your reading more memorable, you also need to use the right side of the brain, which specialises in imagination, creativity, colour and daydreaming. So when you're reading, try to visualise and live the experience. At first you may find this difficult to do. Nevertheless, the very fact that you are trying will improve your powers of imagination and concentration and thus help you remember information better.

Senses

Use all your senses — visual, auditory and tactile: visual for pages, diagrams and pictures; auditory for paraphrasing, recitation and reading aloud; the sense of touch for taking notes and keeping cue cards for revision.

Forming mental images or drawing diagrams or flow charts of key study material will help you to understand it and remember it better. Drawing or note-taking uses the left side of the brain while visualisation draws on the right side of the brain. Thus your ability to recall the information is more than doubled.

People with photographic memory are very rare, but the fact that such people exist proves that our powers of visualisation can be developed to a lesser or greater extent. To improve your memory, live the experiences by engaging as many of the senses as possible. For example, if you are studying company law, picture the process involved when registering a limited liability company. Imagine yourself completing the necessary documentation. Sense the feel of the paper. Picture the inside of Companies House and the bureaucratic hassle you might encounter to get the registration finalised. Experience the emotions. To make the process stand out in your mind even more, imagine you have a ferocious argument with the official at Companies House about some aspect of the procedure.

Discuss the lecture or chapter with a fellow student after reading it. The discussion will give you different perspectives on the topic while holding your concentration and stimulating your mind. It also brings variety into the study approach. Set up formal study sessions or learning sets to discuss course-related topics. Set aside one or two hours each Saturday morning for this purpose.

The mnemonic SHRED will help you recall the key aspects of this section:

- **Seeing**. Visualising the key ideas as you read will help you remember more effectively.

- **Hearing**. Say it out loud for better retention. Not suitable for normal reading, but very useful when you are revising for examinations or preparing for that key presentation.

- **Reporting**. If you have to report back to your boss after attending a course, it will concentrate the mind. Also, if you have to make a presentation of the course content, you are more likely to remember it more effectively.

- **Emotions**. If you feel very strongly about a topic, you are more likely to remember it. Environmentalists are often very emotionally committed as well as being very knowledgeable about their subject. The strong emotions of the first experience of falling in love or of the moments surrounding a car crash help place these events in long-term memory.

- **Doing**. Summarise the key points in the form of a learning map. Rewrite it if necessary. Walk up and down as you revise something. Aristotle (384–322 BC) said that it was "better to exercise intellect than merely possess it". Aristotle founded his own school, the Lyceum. Uniquely, at the Lyceum students would take lessons while walking up and down the grounds.

Association

We remember things if we link or associate them with our previous experience or something that we know already. Relate your professional studies to your work and try to integrate them with your everyday life experience. Apply the questioning technique to build up the necessary links and to engrave the subject matter on your memory. Why is this so? How is this so? When is it so? Where is it so? Who said it? How reliable is the source of the information? What else could be deduced? The more the brain is used, the more memory associations are formed. The more associations are formed, the easier it is to remember previously acquired information, and also to form new associations.

There are three laws of association which you may find useful to know. These are:

- **Law of similarity**. This states that two ideas may be associated if they resemble each other; for example, people with the same name. Also, you are more likely to associate a bus with a car than with an aeroplane. In examinations, students are often asked to show the similarities and differences between various theories.

- **Law of contrast**. This states that two ideas may be associated if they contrast with each other. For example, tall and short, day and night. It is easier to learn the differences between "hot" and "cold" than between "hot" and "warm". The law of similarity and contrast suggests that comparing and contrasting ideas is a very effective way of learning information.

- **Law of contiguity**. This states that two ideas may be associated if they have occurred together. For example, if two important events happened on similar or near enough dates, one may be recalled by reference to the other. We all know that the First World War started in 1914. Frederick Winslow Taylor, the "father of scientific management", died the following year in 1915. Connect the two events and you now have a way of recalling the date of Taylor's death. Similarly, if you want to fix in your mind the date when penicillin first came into use (1941), it may help to think of it becoming available in the second year of the Second World War (1939–1945). It is well known that students should be given their marks as soon after an examination as possible, so that they associate the correct answers with the questions while the examination is still fresh in their minds. Similarly, children should be reprimanded as soon as possible after the relevant incident requiring correction.

Techniques: The PLAN System

The best-known memory techniques can be recalled by the mnemonic PLAN. This stands for:

- **P**lace system

- **L**ink system

- **A**lphabet system

- **N**umber rhyme and number shape.

You won't learn to drive a car merely by reading a book. Similarly, it takes considerable time and practice to get proficient in the PLAN system of memory. Nevertheless your efforts will be more than adequately rewarded by the development of an outstanding memory in your area of expertise. Nothing worthwhile is easy to learn and master. So start now, practise and persevere. However, some of the techniques are easier to learn than others. The following are the details of the PLAN system.

Place System

The basic idea in the place system is to use the items of furniture or equipment in each room in your home as hooks to associate or link things to. The hooks might be door, lamp, window, clock, chair, table, plant, TV, cabinet and fireplace. Associate the items you want to remember with these links. Then when you want to remember them you take a mental walk around your house, picking off the items as you go around.

It is easier to associate items with familiar pegs, which is the advantage of the room system. It is also expandable in relation to the number of rooms and items in each room in your home. The pegs can also be items you encounter on a familiar walk or car journey.

For abstract items, you may have to use substitute concrete words. An example, of this would be, say, the principles of Justice, Liberty and Fraternity. To remember these, think of a judge, the Statue of Liberty and a group of your relatives who have turned up unexpectedly. Visualise the judge sitting on your favourite fireside chair, the Statue of Liberty on top of the TV and your relatives sitting on the sofa. Use the MUSE principle to imprint the items on your memory — movement; unusualness; slapstick and exaggeration. The Place technique is easy to learn and use and is very effective.

Link System

This uses your powers of vivid imagination to associate items together in sequence — just like a train with carriages attached. Again, use the MUSE principle when doing so. In other words, see things in an action-related context; larger than life; millions of them; in a humorous situation; or in colour. As an example, say you want to remember dog, television, pencil and apple. Just picture the dog devouring the TV, the TV with pencils stuck out of the screen and apples with pencils stuck in them. The more vivid and unusual the association, the better you'll recall it. The link system works on the principle that people remember things better in the form of stories. The strength of the images and the logic of the sequence provides the cues for retrieval. The link system is a basic memory technique and is very easy to learn and use. However, it may be unreliable, as it requires you to remember the sequence of events in a story.

Alphabet System

In your early school days you committed to memory the 26 letters of the alphabet. This means you have 26 memory hooks to hang things on. The idea is to invent words to represent each letter of the alphabet and commit these to long-term memory. For example:

- A might be axe
- B might be bee
- C might be sea
- D might be deed
- E might be easel
- F might be effigy
- G might be jeans
- H might be H-bomb
- I might be eye
- J might be jay
- K might be cake
- L might be elbow
- M might be empty
- N might be entrance
- O might be oboe
- P might be pea
- Q might be queue
- R might be artist
- S might be Eskimo
- T might be teapot
- U might be U-boat
- V might be vehicle
- W might be WC

- X might be X-ray
- Y might be wire
- Z might be Zulu.

Some of these may not stick in your mind so you should change them for images more meaningful to you. The words chosen may have a similar sound with the letter for easier recall but this is not essential. Best to select the word with the strongest image that comes to mind and stick with it. So if you want to remember 26 items, you link or associate them with these ready-made hooks. The alphabet system is a good technique for memorising long lists of items in a specific order. It enables you to detect missing items very quickly. It is an effective memory technique, easy to learn and fairly easy to use. However, it does take some time to commit the system to memory.

Number rhyme

The number rhyme is a well-known memory system used in scores of memory books. It is a very simple method of remembering lists of items in a specific order. Items missed will become obvious as gaps in your list. The numbers are represented by things that rhyme with the number. Items to be remembered are then linked to these hooks for recall. It goes like this:

- 1 is gun
- 2 is shoe
- 3 is three
- 4 is door
- 5 is hive
- 6 is sticks
- 7 is heaven
- 8 is gate
- 9 is wine
- 10 is hen.

The same principle of associating items you want to remember with these easily recallable hooks is used. You can use the number rhyme technique to recall knowledge in an entire subject area such as management. Images representing the theories of each management guru can be associated with the images representing the management theorist's name. Their names in turn can be linked to the hooks. The more humorous and vivid the image, the more effectively you will remember it. For example, Frederick Taylor, the father of scientific management, can be visualised discarding his shoes in order to observe workers surreptitiously for a work measurement exercise. Two is shoe and shoe elicits the image of Taylor. Make up your own links and see how you get on! The number rhyme technique is easy to learn, easy to use and is very effective.

Number Shape

In the number system, numbers are represented by images shaped like the number. It may be used to remember a list of things or numbers. It is another example of a peg system. The scheme used might be:

- 1 is a pole

- 2 is a swan

- 3 is a butterfly

- 4 is a sailing boat

- 5 is a sickle

- 6 is a snake rolled up in a form of a six

- 7 is the bow of a ship

- 8 is an hourglass

- 9 is a walking stick

- 10 is a bat and ball.

If you find that these images do not work for you, then change them for something more meaningful to you. As in the number rhyme system, the words are memory hooks on which you can hang the items you want to remember. The number shape technique is a very effective way of remembering lists. You can also use this technique to recall dates or numbers. So to recall 26, you could visualise a swan devouring a snake. It is very easy to learn and use.

Intensity

The more intense your interest in a topic, the more likely you are to remember it. Hobbies are areas that people have a fund of knowledge about because they are interested and naturally review their knowledge.

Develop an interest in your topic for better learning and recall. Read around your topic. At the very least, read an appropriate professional journal and the business pages in the newspapers. Interest creates motivation and counteracts boredom. Integrate what you want to remember into your everyday activities. Information is forgotten quickly if not actively reflected on and used.

Intensity, motivation, interest and confidence are all interlinked. Each reinforces the other. The more success you have, the more confident and motivated you become. Similarly, the more enthusiastic you are about a topic, the better your recall.

Overview

Get an overview of a topic first before you tackle the details. When reading, use the SQ3R approach, as discussed elsewhere. This is sometimes called the "holistic method". The mind likes to get an overview of a topic before it starts filling in the details, just as we tackle a jigsaw puzzle — we look at the illustration and then start working from the outer edges and work our way inwards. We are using a telescopic approach, going from less detail to more detail. Psychologists call this the "gestalt" approach. Of course, learning maps are an application of this idea.

Novelty

In psychology, this is called the Von Restorff effect. We remember things that are unique and outstanding. That's how you only remember the funny or unique incidents of your holiday. The rest is familiar and merges in with many other similar and routine experiences of our lives.

In a list of words, it is the unusual word that stands out and can be recalled. Pop stars often dress in an outrageous fashion to attract attention and make them unique and outstanding — and memorable. In learning maps you can make things stand out by the use of cartoons, colour, two-dimensional figures and symbols.

Types of Memory

The types of memory we have can be recalled by the mnemonic WISE which is illustrated in the following diagram:

TYPES OF MEMORY

| Working |
| Implicit |
| Semantic |
| Episodic |

- **Working memory** is our short-term memory. It enables us to link new ideas with existing experience or stores of knowledge and generate completely novel ideas. Some people refer to it as the "blackboard of the mind". Others compare it to random access memory (RAM), which is the working memory in a personal computer.

- **Implicit**. This is our memory for automatic responses such as driving, typing and tying your shoelace. Barring some major physical or psychological disability, until we die we will remember how to walk, pick up our glass and drink, or sign our name.

- **Semantic**. This is our memory for language, information, rules, facts, concepts and knowledge. Semantic memory allows us to define, order and operate within the world. It helps us remember the countries of the world and their capital cities. It helps us to categorise things as plants or animals and the meaning of the red and green signals on traffic lights.

- **Episodic**. This is our memory for autobiographical details and specific events. When we reminisce, we are using episodic memory. This is the memory evoked by photos from the family album about past events in our lives. Personal recollections of your first day at work, your wedding day and the birth of your first child are calling upon episodic memory. Episodic memory can be recalled quite quickly.

Learning Maps

Wake up your memory by using learning maps for all note-taking and learning situations. The technique of making learning maps can be recalled by the mnemonic CHAIRMAN:

- **Capitals**. Use capital letters. These have greater impact and are clearer to read.

- **Hayfork**. Use the hayfork and fishbone technique.

- **A4 sheet**. For most purposes, the A4 sheet is fine for learning maps. The odd time, depending on the quantity of information you want to include, an A3 sheet might be better.

- **Images**. Brighten up your learning maps with images, drawings, diagrams, cartoons, symbols and colour. Segment or draw coloured lines around major themes.

- **Radiate out**. You start in the centre with your key word and then radiate out from there.

- **Mnemonics**. Using mnemonics on your learning map will help you recall key points better.

- **Attach**. Attach sub-themes to themes and themes to centre.

- **Nouns**. Concrete nouns are best for keywords, as these will unlock your memory.

Advantages of Learning Maps

The advantages of learning maps can be recalled by the mnemonic FRAMEWORK, which is illustrated in the following diagram:

ADVANTAGES OF LEARNING MAPS — FRAMEWORK

Flexible
Recall
Associations
Multisensory Brain
Essence
Word Images
Organised
Reconnaisance
Knowledge of Brain

- **Flexible**. Learning maps can be developed by adding new pieces of information to the appropriate branch. With linear notes, this creates logistical problems. Adding to learning maps is easy and may be brought about through serendipity, serious and pastime reading, discussion, watching television, listening to the radio, observation, experience, research and reflective and critical thought. These additions may be cross-referenced to their original source. Because learning maps are open-ended, students can brainstorm and personalise by adding concepts, ideas, or reactions as lectures are presented. The resultant learning map is a comprehensive, concentrated, conceptualised, integrated, visual and easily digestible overview and keyword summary of a topic.

- **Recall, review and revise**. Rereading of textbooks, study manuals, distance learning units and management consultant's reports is kept to a minimum. Only keywords, associations and images are concentrated on. This gives the reader more time for doing other things. In the long term, learning maps save time, and in preparing for professional and university degrees, especially those done on a part-time basis whilst holding down a full-time job, often with family commitments, time management is critical to success. Psychologists have shown that recall, review and reflection are essential to consolidate information in long-term memory and to optimise learning. Notes in neat lines may be fine as far as essay writing is concerned, but they don't help memory. In a learning map, all the various factors have been brought together to produce more effective note-taking and to enhance recall. A learning map with its keywords, particularly if these have been converted to mnemonics, is much easier to learn than 20 pages of linear notes.

- **Associations**. The node–link relationship on learning maps helps the learner to assimilate new facts and to perceive how detailed information links to the central concept.

- **Multisensory brain**. Learning maps integrate the hearing, seeing and feeling aspects of the brain.

- **Essence**. The overall concept is highlighted in the centre of a learning map, with the hierarchy of ideas evolving from it, providing a clear overview all in the same page. Some people fail examinations not because of insufficient preparation but because they clutter up their minds with detail and are thus unable to identify the key issues — a type of "paralysis by analysis". Effective learning means working smarter rather than harder. It means learning concepts and broad principles rather than cluttering up the mind with details. In memorising anything, it is vital to get an overview so that you understand the broad principles involved before you begin. When information is simply listed, it is difficult to prioritise ideas. It is hard to see relationships, connect ideas, and see the "big picture", and the result is a lot of information with no form or hierarchy of significance. The learning map structure graphically connects all ideas and shows the significance of each in relation to each other and to the centre.

- **Word images**. A picture is worth more than a thousand words. A learning map is a visual aid with panache, impact, originality, style and creativity. The effectiveness of our learning is increased the more senses we use, particularly the visual, auditory and tactile senses. Psychologists tell us that impressions come mostly through the eyes. Therefore, visual stimulation is most important to learning. They have also shown that images linked to words improve recall. Hence the significance of images linked to words in learning maps. Since the ancient Greeks, techniques have been taught using images as an aid to memory. Visualising learning maps in your mind's eye will provide the training and practice to increase your skill at creating mental images.

- **Organised**. Learning maps are a structured way of getting down facts on paper. Just as on a road map, where major roads (key concepts), minor roads (important ideas), and byways (important details) can be easily differentiated by the thickness of lines, codes, dimensions, colours and so on, learning maps use a similar technique to highlight important information. Psychologists have established that organisation is one of the key components of a good memory. Learning maps provide the structure, organisation and context for learning. They link new information to existing knowledge and experience, thereby facilitating comprehension, learning and memory.

- **Reconnaissance**. Learning maps will help you carry out a reconnaissance of text. Effective criminals usually carry out a thorough reconnaissance of the bank they plan to rob. Good drivers use advance organisers by studying road maps. Similarly, learning maps can be used to preview chapters and whole books. Psychological research shows that previewing outlines improves learning and recall by establishing a framework or context for new information.

- **Knowledge of brain**. Learning maps may be an effective way of whole brain learning by integrating both sides of the brain. The use of words and structure involves the left side of the brain, while the use of images and colour involves the right side of the brain. There is increasing evidence that the ability to put thoughts into images as well as words enhances thinking skills and actually improves intelligence.

Disadvantages of Learning Maps

- **Unconventional and time-consuming**. They can be time consuming to create, particularly if using colour and images to support the text. Many people find them unconventional and childish. There is a natural resistance to the concept, as people find it difficult to adapt after a lifetime of linear notes. They also find it difficult to convert words into images and draw the pictures.

- **Map shock**. Some people feel overwhelmed and intimidated by the learning map size and complexity. This may reduce motivation and interfere with learning. Unlike text, there are usually several ways to read a learning map. Although this gives people greater freedom to explore the topic, in some cases it appears to lead to redundant, incomplete or haphazard learning.

- **Practice**. A small minority of people have difficulty grasping and applying learning maps. This may be due to different learning styles. The logistics of actually doing one can be daunting to the novice. In fact, to become really competent requires a lot of practice.

- **The Hawthorne Effect**. There is always the lingering doubt that the success of learning maps may be partially influenced by the Hawthorne Effect. It may be the novelty factor that attracts peoples' attention, provides interest, and motivation and thus leads to enhanced recall. As soon as the novelty value wears off, people may lose interest.

- **Lack of standardisation**. Besides learning maps, there are many approaches to mapping including mind, memory, knowledge, semantic, concept and clustering. Even with learning maps, adherents adopt different styles with different structures, unique links and associations. They may have different views as to what constitute keywords and appropriate images. This personalisation of the technique and lack of standardisation makes comparison and research difficult.

- **Good for key points, poor for details**. Learning maps seem to be better at giving people the "big picture" rather than the detail.

Learning States

The following are some of the aspects that will help you recreate the right state for learning:

- **Positive attitude**. If we have a strong self-belief that we are effective learners, we are more likely to learn.

- **Affirmations**. The subconscious mind believes what you constantly feed it. Feed it with positive messages about your ability to learn, memorise and concentrate. Affirmations should be positive, personal and made in the present tense.

- **Visualisation**. Visualise yourself in situations where you are learning successfully. The stronger and more vivid the pictures the better.

- **Mental rehearsal**. Anticipate successful outcomes by mentally rehearsing them in your head.

- **State-dependent memory**. Memory is often linked to a particular context. What is learned in one place is best recalled in the same place. This phenomenon is well known to the police who often recreate the scene of a crime on television in order to prompt people's memories of events. In an experiment, divers who memorised words underwater had better recall of the words underwater than on dry land.

- **Relaxation**. You are more likely to learn when in a state of relaxed alertness. Stress inhibits learning and memory.

Concentration

The barriers to concentration include:

- **Haste**. If a job is worth doing it is worth doing well. Give the task the commitment and time it deserves.

- **Fatigue** may be due to lack of sleep or overwork.

- **Boredom**. If a topic does not meet your need, it will hold no interest for you.

- **Distractions** may be internal, such as preoccupations, or external, such as noise.

The CONSENT Model of Concentration

An overview is given in the following diagram:

CONCENTRATION — CONSENT MODEL

Chunk
Ongoing Recall
Needs
Self-talk
Eliminate Distractions
Now
Targets

- **C**hunk. Divide and conquer. Instead of reading a book, read chapters. Instead of reading chapters, read sections and paragraphs. This chunking has the psychological effect of making the task more manageable. Your span of attention is about 20 minutes, so you should chunk your time in blocks of 20 minutes, taking short breaks in between.

- **O**ngoing recall. Spend up to 50 per cent of your time recalling. Take notes, preferably in learning map form, at the recall stage and use these for review. Adopt the SQ3R approach to reading tasks: Survey, Question, Read, Recall and Review. Generate images for keywords, as visual memory lasts longer than verbal memory.

- **Needs**. Identify why the reading meets your needs. What benefits will accrue to you as a result of reading the book? Focusing on how the reading will meet your needs will create interest and motivation while reading the text.

- **Self-talk**. Attitude and self-perception is an important aspect of good concentration. We are what we think we are. The more you believe that your concentration is good, the better your concentration will become. Affirm to yourself, "My concentration is very focused"; "I am totally concentrated"; "My powers of concentration are excellent". Feed these statements into your mind over a period of time so that it becomes part of your subconscious. Relax and use repetition each day to imprint affirmations and images into your subconscious.

- **Eliminate internal and external distractions**. To eliminate internal distractions, relax, know your biorhythms and plan your reading accordingly, verbalise and visualise what you want, set specific realistic goals and break your goals into manageable sub-goals. To eliminate external distractions, create a proper work environment, read in a quiet place or with baroque background music, organise your workspace, use good lighting and sit in a comfortable chair.

- **Now**. Do it now! Procrastination is the thief of time. Procrastination has been defined as the automatic postponement of an unpleasant task, for no good reason. Get down to the task straight away. Take a point of view or perspective as you read to enhance your recall.

- **Targets**. Read with a purpose. Specify your learning objectives at the outset and self-test at the end of the reading session. Reading with specific objectives in mind directs attention and facilitates comprehension of relevant information. Have start and finish times for your reading session. "That which can be done at any time, rarely gets done at all."

Summary

Accelerated learning is all about improving your ability to learn and pick up skills quickly. Some of the approaches covered in this chapter were:

Speed-reading. This consists of two aspects: one to improve your efficiency at reading, such as adopting some of the speed-reading advice given; and the other to improve your effectiveness at reading, such as using the SQ3R approach.

Power memory. MEMORISATION was the power memory model discussed. This stands for:

- **M**nemonics
- **E**xpectation
- **M**ind maps
- **O**rganisation
- **R**epetition
- **I**magination
- **S**enses
- **A**ssociation
- **T**echniques of memory
- **I**ntensity
- **O**verview
- **N**ovelty.

The types of memory can be recalled by the mnemonic WISE:

- **W**orking memory
- **I**mplicit memory
- **S**emantic memory
- **E**pisodic memory

Learning maps. How to compile learning maps can be recalled by using the mnemonic CHAIRMAN:

- **C**apitals
- **H**ayfork
- **A**4 images
- **I**mages
- **R**adiate out
- **M**nemonics
- **A**ttach ideas to centre
- **N**ouns for better recall.

The advantages and disadvantages of learning maps were discussed in some detail.

Concentration or focused attention is a must for learning. The key aspects of concentration can be recalled by the mnemonic CONSENT:

- **C**hunk
- **O**ngoing recall
- **N**eeds
- **S**elf-talk
- **E**liminate distractions
- **N**ow
- **T**argets.

CHAPTER 6 LEARNING MAP

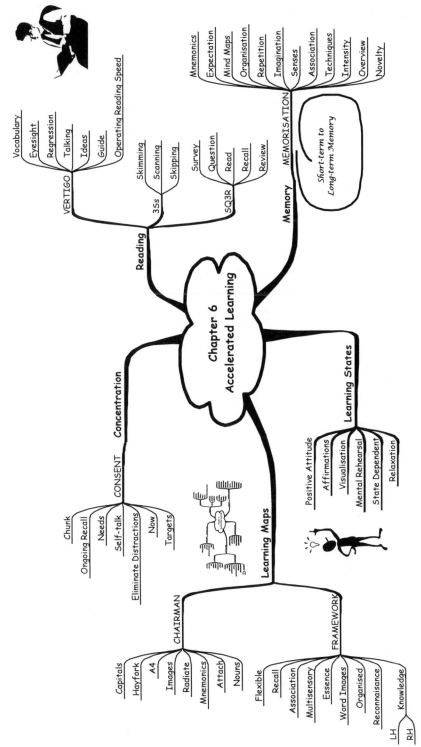

Chapter 6 Accelerated Learning

Reading

VERTIGO
- Vocabulary
- Eyesight
- Regression
- Talking
- Ideas
- Guide
- Operating Reading Speed

3Ss
- Skimming
- Scanning
- Skipping

SQ3R
- Survey
- Question
- Read
- Recall
- Review

Memory

MEMORISATION
- Mnemonics
- Expectation
- Mind Maps
- Organisation
- Repetition
- Imagination
- Senses
- Association
- Techniques
- Intensity
- Overview
- Novelty

Short-term to Long-term Memory

Concentration

CONSENT
- Chunk
- Ongoing Recall
- Needs
- Self-talk
- Eliminate Distractions
- Now
- Targets

Learning Maps

CHAIRMAN
- Capitals
- Hayfork
- A4
- Images
- Radiate
- Mnemonics
- Attach
- Nouns

FRAMEWORK
- Flexible
- Recall
- Association
- Multisensory
- Essence
- Word Images
- Organised
- Reconnaisance
- Knowledge
  - LH
  - RH

Learning States
- Positive Attitude
- Affirmations
- Visualisation
- Mental Rehearsal
- State Dependent
- Relaxation

7

Time Management for Learning

"I would I could stand on a busy corner, hat in hand, and
beg people to throw me all their wasted hours."
— Bernard Berenson

♦ *Why is time management so important?*

♦ *Why is time management important to career planning?*

♦ *What are timelines?*

♦ *How can I find time for learning?*

♦ *What is the Pareto Principle?*

♦ *What is the time management model?*

♦ *What are biorhythms?*

♦ *How can I become more efficient?*

Objectives of Time Management

Managing your time is so important for learning and self-development, particularly if you are studying for a third-level qualification on your own time. To become a good time manager, you must have the desire and determination to acquire the right time-effective habits. You must take the decision to adopt these habits and you must have the determination to stick with them. If you want to succeed in learning, you must have written objectives. Objectives keep you motivated by giving you a sense of direction and purpose.

The importance of objectives in time management are:

- They help you achieve goals. Learning objectives direct your attention and focus your concentration on what needs to be done.

- They keep you in control. You know what you have to do and you set up an implementation plan to do it.

- They reduce stress in your life by eliminating procrastination.

- They prioritise important areas of your life. Meeting the objectives of your personal development plan is your long-term goal. Meeting your daily learning objectives is your short-term goal.

- They help you progress in your career. Unless you have objectives and a personal development plan, you are unlikely to achieve your career goals. It is too important to leave to chance.

- To balance work, play and learning time, and help you enjoy life more. Time management is all about getting the mix right. You want to achieve your goals, but at the same time you want to keep mentally, emotionally and physically fit.

- To generally help you become more efficient and effective. Time is money. So you don't want to waste time. Making time count is more important than counting time.

Career Planning

Failure to plan is planning to fail. Set down your career goals. Decide how you are going to achieve them. It will probably be by a combination of getting the right experience, acquiring the right qualifications, being guided by a good mentor, and making the right career choices at the right time.

Look back at the career stages outlined in Chapter 5. Plan now so that when you look back in years to come you won't regret the past. Career planning is about:

- Seeing the big picture;

- Planning significant events in your life;

- Acquiring the right experience and the right qualifications;

- Being guided by a good mentor;

- Knowing where you want to be at different stages of your life;

- Planning your career moves;

- Being in the right place at the right time.

Don't wait around for other people to do things for you. If you do you will be disappointed. People have their own interests at heart rather than yours. Determine the direction of your own career and make it work for you.

Timelines

This is the way we store pictures, sounds and feelings of our past, present and future. Some people live in the future, all the time talking about what they are going to do. Other people have difficulty thinking further ahead than the next few days. Some people live in the past, enjoy reminiscing and their memories are as real as current experiences. Others live in the here and now, enjoying all the pleasures of life without either regrets about the past or worries about the future. Most people in western cultures see the past on their left and the future on their right. This is called "through time". "Through time" people are good at keeping appointments, deadlines are important to them and they find it harder to stay in the moment. In the west, we are governed by the clock.

The other timeline is called "in time". Here the timeline stretches from front to back so that the past is behind you. This is sometimes called Arabic time. It is prevalent in eastern cultures, but there are also people in the west who operate within this time-frame. These people generally do not place the same importance on aspects of time management such as deadlines, appointments and time-keeping as most of us do. Their sense of urgency is much less than ours. This is often a source of frustration for people in the west when they are doing business with people from the east. For them, time happens now and time schedules are not important.

Where and how you store your timeline influences the way you think and how good you are likely to be at time management. People who live in the present do not worry about the future and are likely to be poor at planning or thinking ahead. Observation confirms that it is the same people who are late for meetings and appointments all the time. They are likely to be "in time" people rather than "through time" people and this accounts for their poor timekeeping.

Thoughts can influence the way you see time. For example, some people see the future as big and bright and the past as dim and distant. Or the opposite might be the case, which explains why some people are attracted to the past or the future. The phrase "the future looks bright" can be a literal description of the future for some people. On the other hand, the phrase "putting the past behind you", can be an exact description of where some people's thoughts appear to be.

By becoming aware of your thoughts about time, you will become aware how your timelines operate. You can alter the structure of your timeline. You can change the size and intensity of the images you see and thus change your perception of time. Engage in visualisation exercises to do this. For example, a future event can be visualised as more attractive and thus become a more compelling goal. A bad memory can be reduced to the level at which it becomes insignificant and loses its power.

Finding Time for Learning

Time availability analysis is about finding time for work, family home life and learning activities. The following diagram illustrates the process.

WEEKLY TIME AVAILABILITY ANALYSIS

Activity	Hours
Sleeping	56
Commuting	10
Working	40
Personal Needs	20
Balance	42
Total	*168*

There are 168 hours in a week. You spend 56 hours in bed (7 x 8). You spend about 50 hours in work and in commuting. You spend about 20 hours eating and attending to personal needs. This leaves a balance of 42 hours for recreation, relationships and personal development. This is about six hours per day for recreation and personal development. How much of this time should you devote to study and personal development? If you are studying for a degree or professional qualification part-time, you would need to devote about three hours per day. This is a big commitment of your time and you will need to be highly organised to do so. Make sure you build in time for rest and relaxation.

Planning means having objectives and working to timetables. Drawing up a timetable for study will concentrate your mind on what subjects you need to attend to, how much time you need to devote to each and when you should be studying. The amount of time devoted to a particular subject depends on the difficulty and interest of the subject for you. The more difficult a subject is and the less interest you have in it, the more time you should devote to studying it. The following is a typical timetable:

Subject	Mon	Tues	Wed	Thurs	Fri	Sat	Sun
A	7–8	7–8	Rest	7–8	7–8	As needed	
B	8–9	8–9	Rest	8–9	8–9	As needed	
C	9–10	9–10	Rest	9–10	9–10	As needed	

The following are some of the principles you should keep in mind when designing a good timetable:

- Decide on the number of hours for study each week. Consult the syllabus to see the range of topics within the subject and estimate how long each topic will require. Consult with the course director for guidance.

- Space the hours over the week. Remember to leave at least one day per week free for recreation.

- Decide on the time of day for study. People pursuing careers usually have only evenings and weekends. Be aware of your biorhythms. An hour in the morning may be worth more than its equivalent at night-time because your mind may be more alert. However, if you are one of those people who never reaches peak mental performance before 11.00 a.m., then early morning study is not for you!

- Decide on the length of each study session. Most people prefer to study in one-hour periods even though the span of concentration is about 20 minutes. So take plenty of breaks for rest, review and reflection. The primacy and recency effect in memory states that you remember things better at the start and end of a session. In between, you are inclined to forget unless you make the topic unique and outstanding. Introduce variety into your time by reading, reviewing and doing things. This suggests that the more breaks you have the better. Start each session with a review of the previous night's work. End each session with a review of the current work.

- Before you start to study, ask yourself two questions: "Why am I studying this subject?" and "What do I want to learn about it?" Study is always more effective if you have a purpose and you understand what you are trying to achieve.

- Have variety in your timetable. A change of subject will refresh your mind. Study the most difficult subject first, when your mind is most alert.

You should have learning objectives for each study session. This concentrates the mind. After each session self-test to ensure that you have in fact met your learning objectives. This prevents you moving on before mastering the learning task at hand.

Procrastination

Putting things off for a future time when you should be doing them now. This idea is clearly made in the following well-known verse:

> *He slept beneath the moon,*
> *He basked beneath the sun.*
> *He lived a life of going to do,*
> *But died with nothing done.*
> *— Anon*

Some of the causes of procrastination have been identified as:

- **Being overwhelmed by a task**. In the case of a large report, the approach might be to divide and conquer: break the report into manageable sections, within each section do one page at a time. Find a quiet place to do it. Use a learning map to gather your thoughts, create a momentum and prevent writer's block.

- **Unclear goals**. Work to plans supported by targets and clear deadlines.

- **Fear of failure**.

- **Tendency to overcommit**. This means taking on more than you should. Delegate or become more assertive. Being able to say "no" may lighten your workload.

- **Addiction to cramming**. Leaving things to the last minute and then putting yourself under undue pressure is a common occurrence with students preparing for examinations, who feel they can fatten the pig before the fair. In reality this is a disastrous policy. Working to plans, schedules and timetables should prevent this.

- **Unpleasant tasks**. Get stuck in before you start to rationalise on all the reasons why you shouldn't do it.

Proactive versus Reactive

Proactive people are those who plan ahead. Reactive people are those who react to situations; their work is dictated by the exigencies of the situation. Time management is all about balance. It means not being too extreme in the style we adopt. For example, you could plan and schedule everything and leave no time for emergencies that will inevitably arise. Allowing time for contingencies should be part of your time management approach. On the other hand, you might fail to plan anything and finish up with no sense of direction, priorities or purpose. This leads to inefficiency and wasted effort.

Some people never give a thought to tomorrow. They live in the here and now and enjoy the present moment. They may enjoy the excitement of an unplanned day. Others would not know what to do with the extra time saved if they became more efficient. In some organisations, efficiency may be rewarded with more work. However, you need to know where you are going if you want to achieve your targets.

People who are focused on the future may produce the opposite effect. If they feel that everything has to be planned to the last detail, they may fail to enjoy the moment. You need a bit of flexibility in your life. So a balanced approach is needed.

Pareto Principle

Sometimes called the 80/20 rule, ABC analysis, or the law of the critical few and the trivial many. Twenty per cent of what you do accounts for 80 per cent of your results. Thus, 80 per cent of your time may be spent on activities that may not be very useful. Categorise tasks as:

- **Must do**. Probably account for up to 75 per cent of your work tasks. These are non-discretionary items that are prescribed by the organisation as really essential and central to your job.

- **Should do**. Probably account for up to 20 per cent of your work tasks. These may be important but not urgent. Schedule them for a free time in the future.

- **Nice to do**. Probably account for up to 5 per cent of your work tasks. Consider eliminating these from your workload. These are often referred to as the "do or dump" category.

Identify the key result areas of your job, as these are the priorities. Why are you on the payroll? What could you do right now that would make a real difference to your job? Consider important versus urgent tasks. Do what's important and urgent. Dump or delegate those tasks of low importance and low urgency.

Time Management Model

Importance: how does this help me achieve my overall purpose? Urgency: when does it need to be done? The following is the time management model:

TIME MANAGEMENT MODEL

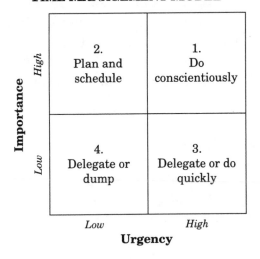

1. These are items that are of high importance and high urgency. Do immediately but give them sufficient time and effort. Examples would include revision before a forthcoming examination, or assignments and projects which are due to a deadline.

2. These are items of high importance but low urgency. These include scheduling, setting deadlines, and allocating time for learning activities. These are part of your long-term commitment to lifelong learning. You may need to acquire word-processing skills to type up that thesis which you have to do in 12 months' time. You may need to formulate a research question for your thesis and research the topic. You need to source out books and research material to support your thesis. This you can do anytime within the next six months. These eventually become category one items if ignored.

3. These are items of low importance and high urgency. You should do these immediately or delegate to someone else to do them for you. These may include photocopies of research articles

that you have collected to support your thesis. These need to be categorised and filed away for future reference. Lecture handouts and college syllabus and procedures need to be filed away systematically so that you can find them when you need them.

4. These are items of low importance and low urgency. You should delegate these or dump them. These might include keeping your study area organised and clear of clutter, including dumping those papers that are not necessary to your purpose or that you no longer require. A magpie instinct will lead to disorganisation so that you will be unable to find important items when you need to.

Approaches to Study

*   **Individual**. Some people prefer to study on their own. This can be very lonely and requires a lot of commitment to be successful. However, some individuals find that this is the most productive use of their time.

*   **Group**. Study groups or learning sets that meet on a regular basis can be a very productive way of studying. You may find that having other people to consult with and compare notes with can save a lot of study time. Learning sets can provide emotional support and motivation when the going gets tough.

*   **Study environment**. Find a quiet place for study. If you have difficulty finding a quiet place for study at home, then the office at work may be a suitable location. Psychologically, the office is associated with work and this may put you in the right mood for concentrated study. One memory aid involves making the surroundings in which you remember material similar to those in which you learned the material. For this reason, soccer coaches require players to practise under conditions similar to those of an actual game. Students often find it helpful to study in the room where they will be taking the examination.

*   **Be organised**. Sit upright on a hard chair at your desk. Sitting on a sofa is not the best way to study productively! The room temperature should be warm enough to keep you comfortable

and cold enough to keep your alert. Have your study books and materials close at hand. Study one thing at a time. Remove all distractions. Attend to the current lesson. Put finished work aside and out of sight.

The PASS Model

Your aim is to PASS your examinations. PASS is a mnemonic which stands for:

PASS MODEL

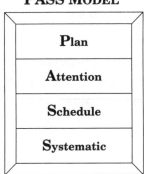

- **Plan**. Planning is just as important in your studies as it is in your business career. Planning includes having long-term and short-term objectives, timetables, schedules and measuring your actual performance against targets and learning objectives. Use "to do" lists each day. Build in time for reflection in your day. Take time to read, review and reflect each day. Constantly ask yourself the question: "Am I making the best possible use of my time right now?"

- **Attention**. Develop your powers of concentration, as discussed elsewhere in this book. Develop listening skills. Listening is a skill which improves with practice. As you listen to the lecturer, try to summarise the key points in your head. Better still, put them on paper in the form of a learning map.

- **Schedule** time for work and recreation. A balanced life will keep your mind and body healthy. This is where your time management skills come in.

- **Systematic**. This means being methodical in your approach and sticking to your plans, schedules and timetables.

Balancing Recreation and Study Time

Efficient use of time will give you more time for work, recreation and personal development.

- **Recreation time**. Balance and moderation should be your objective. Make time for leisure activities and relationships. Look after your health. Your health is your wealth! Have a proper diet and take plenty of exercise.

- **Study and personal development time**. Lifelong learning should be your goal. Be a perpetual student. Work on yourself, listen to educational tapes, watch educational videos, do CD-ROM courses on your computer and attend seminars. Learn a new skill each year.

Biorhythms

This is your biological clock. It generally coincides with the 24-hour day. Its most obvious manifestation is the regular cycle of sleeping and waking. Also, body temperature and the concentration of hormones that influence mood and behaviour vary over the day. Alteration of habit, such as shift work and air travel, may put your biorhythms out of phase, causing malaise until it has time to adjust. It is easy to calculate your biorhythms. There are electronic and mechanical biorhythm calculators available. There are also software packages available for your home computer.

There is also an unproven theory that humans are governed by three biorhythms:

- **Intellectual (33 days)**. This rhythm is believed to originate in the brain. In the first half of the cycle, a person is able to think more quickly and clearly and memory operates more efficiently. In the second half, the person finds learning more difficult, thinking less clearly and precisely. As in the next two, the intellectual rhythm follows a predictable rise and fall waveform.

- **Emotional (28 days)**. This appears to originate in the nervous system and shows itself in emotional changes and degrees of sensitivity. During the rising part of the cycle, creativity is greatest and the person is more optimistic and cheerful. On the downswing, there is a tendency towards negativity and irritation.

- **Physical (23 days)**. This rhythm is believed to be rooted in the action of muscle fibres. It influences physical strength, endurance, energy levels, resistance to infection and self-confidence.

Certain days in each cycle are regarded as "critical", even more so if one such day coincides with that of another cycle.

Are you an owl or a lark? What are your best times for physical activity, mental concentration, dealing with others, study and relaxation? Some people find that for study an hour early in the morning is worth more than two hours at night. Other people find they do not wake up fully until about 11 a.m. Many people find that they are inclined to become drowsy in the afternoon and pick up again after 7 p.m. Whatever your biorhythms, you will need to build your learning and personal development activities around times when you are most alert.

Administrative Efficiency

The more efficient and effective you are at doing your job, the more time you will have available for learning and recreation. Efficiency is doing things right; effectiveness is doing the right things. Ask yourself: "Although I'm doing the job right, am I doing the right job?" The right job is one that puts you further along the road to meeting your objectives. In other words, you are working smarter rather than harder. The ideas of administrative efficiency can also be applied to your learning activities and personal development programme. Your aim is to control your work rather than let your work control you! Remember Parkinson's Law: work expands to fill the time available for its completion. The following are some ideas to save time:

- **Keep a time log**. This will help you analyse your time so that you know exactly how it was spent. Spend some time at the end of each day reviewing your time log to see if you could be using your time more effectively. Your diary may serve this purpose.

- **Organise your desk**. Remove distractions. Clear your desk. Concentrate on the job at hand. Batch your tasks. This idea takes advantage of the learning curve phenomenon and saves time. If you try to do too many things at the same time, you get overwhelmed and stressed. Get finished jobs out of the way.

- **Do one thing at a time**. If a job is too large, then it should be broken up into small chunks. Then concentrate on doing each small chunk rather than the complete task. Remember the old saying: "Life is hard by the yard, but by the inch it's a cinch."

- **Operate an efficient filing system**. Weed out things that you don't refer to or need. Organise the most frequently referred to files together. Keep these close at hand. This will save on retrieval time.

- **Plan your phone calls**. Do you need to make it? Would an e-mail be just as effective and less time-consuming? What is the purpose of your phone call? Decide what you are going to say and what information you need to get. Be organised. Have relevant documentation and files close at hand. Determine beforehand how much time you intend to spend on the call. Batch your outside phone calls. Allocate a certain time during the day for making calls. You can also batch incoming calls, if appropriate, by a judicious use of voice mail.

- **Develop a systematic procedure for handling your post**. If you can deal with correspondence straight away, do so. Otherwise, you may revisit it and handle the same correspondence several times.

- **Learn as you go**. Use travel time as learning time. Listen to educational tapes on your personal stereo and in your car, study cue cards or read a good management book while waiting for appointments. In a year or two, by using your time effectively like this you could study the equivalent of a university course in your discipline.

- **Personal efficiency**. Learn time management, speed-reading, memory skills, learning maps, and effective writing skills. The more organised and efficient you are at a personal level, the more time you will have to do the things that you want to do. Research has found that managers spend up to 80 per cent of their time communicating. This would suggest the importance of developing communication skills such as report writing, presentation skills, listening and empathy. Network with work colleagues, friends in other organisations, professional bodies and personal friends to get things done quickly.

- **Travel wisely**. In modern times, travel is something that can be a great time-waster and a major source of stress. How much time do you spend travelling? How can you save time? How much time is wasted moving around your offices or site? So ask yourself: Is the journey necessary? If so, why? Consider whether the business could be done by letter, telephone or e-mail. If the journey is necessary, can you combine two or more trips in the one journey?

The LEADS System

Draw up an action list. Prioritise. Do, delegate, delay or dump. Do those things that are urgent and important. Delegate those things that are appropriate and within the capacity of your staff. Delay those that are not urgent. Dump those that are neither urgent nor important. Next to the dog, the wastepaper basket is a man's best friend. On your "to do" list, cross off items you have attended to. This will give you a feeling of completion and satisfaction.

Doing skills are not particularly difficult. All you need to do is apply effort to what needs to be done instead of putting it off. If you do procrastinate then it may be worthwhile to understand why you do so. It may be the type of person that you are or that your motivation is weak. LEADS is a mnemonic which summaries the "do list" approach. The following diagram illustrates the approach:

LEADS SYSTEM

- **List** tasks to be done at the start of the day or at the end of the previous day.

- **Estimate** the time each task should take. Set yourself realistic deadlines.

- **Allow** buffer time for unforeseen problems. Everything takes longer than you think and if anything can go wrong it will. So build in contingency time.

- **Decide** priorities.

- **Scan** the schedule at the end of the day and bring forward unfinished tasks.

Ideally, you should complete your work schedule each day. However, unforeseen circumstances can upset the best-laid plans. Nevertheless, unfinished business can be like a weight around your neck. This can be stressful. There are enormous benefits in being able to complete your work schedule each day without bringing work home to complete and without having to face a backlog the following day. In fact, it is a good idea to set clear boundaries between work and home and bringing work home should only be necessary in very exceptional circumstances.

Curiosity and a willingness to challenge your existing ways of working and organisational systems and procedures is necessary if you are to develop new and better ways of doing things. You should develop a philosophy of continuous improvement and getting it right first time. Develop some expertise in creativity skills and organisation and methods to help you in your quest for excellence.

Dealing with Others

Other people are probably the greatest consumers of your time. Some people may just waste your time. They believe in wasting everybody else's time as well as their own. They may be casual callers who want to discuss social or sporting events with you. If you are busy, then you have got to be assertive with such people. However, you don't want to cause offence, so you must handle such occasions with great sensitivity and diplomacy.

Meetings are another great source of wasted time if they are not organised and run properly. You should ask yourself the following questions about meetings that you are invited to attend:

- Do they have set time limits? Is there a clear start and finish time? If not, why not?

- Is the purpose of the meeting clear?

- Is your presence essential? Is your presence at the entire meeting essential or could you just attend for the items that are relevant to you? Could you delegate it to one of your staff?

- Will the meeting be well run? Is there an agenda and a competent chairperson in charge?

- Are times allocated to items on the agenda in relation to their importance?

- Are responsibilities for outcomes assigned and followed through?

Time Contract

To make time management part of your life, you should commit yourself to the idea. Draw up an agreement on the following lines to help you implement your time management plan.

"I agree to make full use of my time by:

- Planning quiet times for reflection and long-term planning;

- Balancing my life by setting time aside for family, friends, and personal development;

- Setting time limits for meetings;

- Controlling interruptions;

- Keeping a time log for feedback and corrective action;

- Taking an active interest in the development of my staff;

- Delegating."

Summary

Learning objectives help you focus your concentration on what needs to be done. Unless you have objectives and a personal development plan, you are unlikely to achieve your goals.

Think about the typical successful management career cycle and plan your own. Don't let it happen by chance. Take responsibility for your own career.

Timelines are an interesting idea in that they might help us understand why we have a certain attitude to time. "Through time" people perceive the future and past as more important than the present. They are good at time management. "In time" people perceive the here and now as more important that the future. They are poor at time management.

A time availability analysis will help you to identify the time you have available for personal development and formal study. You will use your time more effectively if you have objectives and work to timetables.

Procrastination is the thief of time. Being aware of the reasons why you procrastinate may help you overcome the problem.

The Pareto Principle is the law of the critical few and the trivial many. This technique helps you to identify the important issues on which you should be spending most of your time.

The time management model analyses tasks into four categories:

- High importance and high urgency

- High importance and low urgency

- Low importance and high urgency

- Low importance and low urgency.

You may decide to study on your own or in groups, depending on your individual preference. Choose a study place that is quiet and suitable for your purpose. Your biorhythms influence the effectiveness of your study. You should study at those times when you are most alert.

The PASS model for study was discussed. This is a mnemonic which stands for:

- **P**lanning

- **A**ttention

- **S**chedule

- **S**ystematic

The more efficient and effective you are at doing your job, the more time you will have available for learning and recreation. Many approaches to becoming more administratively efficient were discussed, as well as drawing up a personal contract for time management.

CHAPTER 7 LEARNING MAP

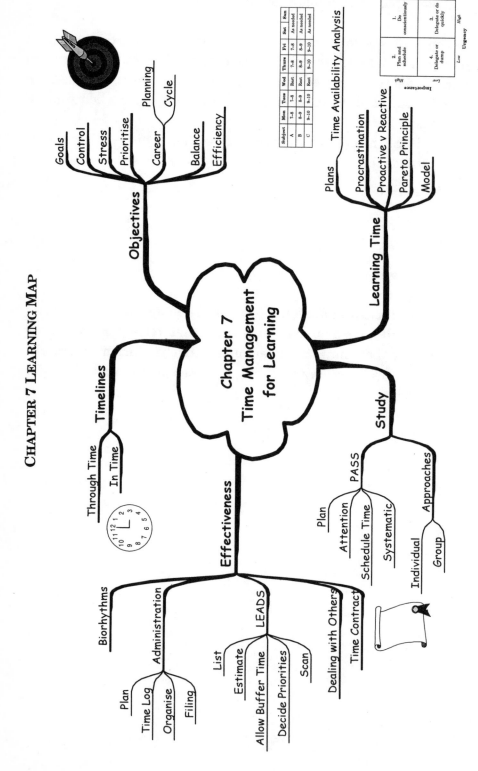

8

Academic and Business Writing

"Anything that is written to please the author is worthless." — Blaise Pascal

---

♦ *What are the six Cs of effective writing?*

♦ *What are the barriers to effective writing?*

♦ *How do I tackle a thesis?*

♦ *What is the best structure for a thesis?*

♦ *What do examiners look for?*

♦ *How do I structure reports?*

Factors Influencing Readability

The following are some of the factors that will determine how readable your writing is:

1. The average number of words in a sentence;

2. The number of commonly understood words;

3. The average number of syllables in the words;

4. The number of long complex sentences;

5. The number of abstract ideas;

6. The use of passive rather than active words;

7. The use of negative words rather than positive words.

Six Cs of Effective Writing

The six Cs of effective writing are:

1. Clear

2. Concise

3. Complete

4. Concrete

5. Correct

6. Coherent.

Let's now explore each of these further.

Be Clear

Avoid clichés, slang, jargon and "commercialese". Your ambition should be to make your writing a "good read". You should write in clear English. Know the exact meaning of words and pick the right ones for the job in hand. Become aware of words that are poorly understood, confused with other words and hence used incorrectly. Also, beware of words that are overused.

Be Concise

Avoid verbosity. Use short sentences in preference to long sentences, short words in preference to long words. Average sentence length should be about 17 words. However, vary the length of your sentences for effect. One-syllable words should make up about 70 per cent of your writing. Use plain words rather than flowery words. Use "start" rather than "commenced" and "end" rather than "terminated". Avoid the overuse of adjectives and adverbs. Avoid repetition and the use of redundant phrases such as "this point in time" — use "now" instead. Avoid clichés or hackneyed phrases. They only serve to irritate. Examples include: "cutting off your nose to spite your face"; "in this day and age"; "at the drop of a hat".

Be Complete

Your writing should be comprehensive, conclusions justified and quantified if appropriate. The conclusions should follow logically from findings and the recommendations should follow on from the conclusions. Problems should be identified and analysed, and derived solutions soundly based.

Be Concrete

Use familiar, concrete words rather than abstract words. Use concrete words such as "rain" rather than abstract ones such as "bad weather". Use "red" rather than "colour". Use "hatred" rather than "emotion". Don't write in a roundabout verbose fashion; get quickly to the point. Your aim should be to enlighten rather than confuse. Churchill (1874–1965) was a master in the use of concrete words and colourful speech. On becoming Prime Minister, he said: "I have nothing to offer but blood, toil, tears and sweat." On another occasion, he said: "We must have a better word than 'prefabricated'. Why not use 'ready-made'?"

Be Correct

Your writing should be factually correct and consistent. Common errors include illogical statements, tautology, spelling, grammar and punctuation. Do not contradict points made elsewhere in your writing. Tautology is saying the same thing twice but using different words such as "free gratis and for nothing". Become aware of the words you often misspell so that you can take corrective action to avoid them in the future. Know the basic rules of grammar and be able to handle full stops, semicolons and other punctuation correctly. As a writer, these are some of the tools of your trade.

Be Coherent

Your writing should be logical and structured. If a sentence reads, sounds and looks as if there is something wrong with it, then there probably is. Develop good presentation skills. Observe the layout of good articles and books. Similarly, you should know how to lay out your work in the best possible manner to achieve your purpose and to make your writing user-friendly. Each paragraph should be introduced with a topic sentence, which contains the main idea of the paragraph. Transition words such as "furthermore" and "therefore" may be used to link points made in the paragraph. The unity of paragraphs should be maintained by avoiding contradictions, digressions and irrelevancies. It is important to maintain the theme of the paragraph.

Barriers to Effective Writing

These include ambiguity, jargon, style, structure and punctuation.

- *Ambiguity* is using words that do not express your meaning. Pick the right word for the job.

- *Jargon* is using business terms or technical terms that may not be known to the reader. Avoid if at all possible or else explain.

- *Style* would include a preference for long words and sentences that hinder comprehension for the reader. Your job should be to make the writing as user-friendly as possible.

- *Structure* includes layout and presentation. Use plenty of signposts such as headings and subheadings to make the job of reading as easy and as pleasant a task as possible.

- *Punctuation*: putting commas in the wrong place can change the meaning of a sentence completely. Make sure your punctuation achieves the effect you desire.

Enhancing Text

Use the following with bold or italic style as appropriate:

- Headings

- Subheadings

- Indentations

- Underlining

- Listing points

- Numbering of points

- Bullet points.

Research Model for a Thesis

The following diagram gives a brief overview of the research process:

RESEARCH MODEL FOR A THESIS

Define Problem
Review Literature
Formulate Hypothesis
Research Design
Implement
Interpret
Report

- **Define the research problem or question**. A problem well defined is a problem half-solved. You need to avoid getting the right answer to the wrong question. Don't confuse the symptoms with the problem. Formulate your initial research question, research objective and research proposal. Research objectives specify information needs. For the research project to be successful, the research problem must be converted into clear and precise research objectives. The research proposal is a written statement of the research design drawn up to investigate the research question. The research proposal will allow your tutor to evaluate your proposed research and see if any changes are needed. Most research proposals will include purpose of the research, research design, data-gathering techniques, budget and time schedule. What is your initial hypothesis? A hypothesis is your tentative proposition, which you will need to verify through further investigation. It acts as a guide to the researcher, as it suggests the method to be followed in studying the problem. In many cases, hypotheses are hunches that you have about the existence of a relationship between variables.

- **Review literature** to see what is available to support your hypothesis. Carry out a preliminary review of books, magazines, newspapers, research reports and the Internet. Do these support your hypothesis? The purpose of the exploratory research is to narrow the scope of the research progressively and nail down specific research objectives. It will also show how feasible the project is.

- **Formulate or reformulate your hypothesis** based on the findings of your initial research. Firm up on your research question, research objective, and research proposal.

- **Research design** comprises two aspects: the literature review and the empirical research. Both are very important aspects of your work. You will now research the literature pertinent to your research question. The empirical research will be done in-company to support your thesis.

- **Implement**. You can carry out the literature research and empirical research concurrently or as opportunity presents itself. In any event, you should be doing one or the other at any one time. It is important that you are constantly making progress towards your goal of completing your thesis by the required time. Empirical research may involve designing questionnaires, interviewing staff or studying archival information in the company. Write as you go (WAYGO). You need to keep complete records of everything you do as you do your research. Don't rely on your memory!

- **Interpret**. You will probably need to analyse the information collected and classify in the format that suits your purpose. Tables, graphs, bar charts and diagrams may be useful. You will need to draw findings, conclusions and recommendations based on your literature and empirical research. How do the two match up?

- **Report**. This is your thesis and should follow accepted practice and college guidelines as regards presentation and layout.

What Examiners Want

Generally, examiners want you to display competency in the literature and empirical research, presentation and layout, and in your findings, conclusions and recommendations. More specifically, they are interested in:

- **Abstract**. This should include the research question, the research methods used and a summary of findings, conclusions and recommendations.

- **Introduction**. This should include a clear definition of the problem. It should state the key issues and give a brief overview of the thesis.

- **Body**. This should show logical development. The material chosen from the literature research should be relevant and serve your purpose. It should demonstrate that you have read widely to find information to back up your thesis. Your empirical research should be sensible, practical and support your thesis. You should defend the reasons why you chose particular research methods and give reasons for rejecting alternative methods. You should give the advantages and disadvantages of the chosen method. Theoretical models may be drawn on to justify your thesis. Generally, your work should show creativity, insight, innovation and originality.

- **Conclusions**. This is probably the most important part of your thesis and deserves the most attention when preparing. Together with the abstract, it may be the only part of your thesis that is thoroughly read. It should show and highlight the significance of your findings, conclusions and recommendations. You should demonstrate an understanding of the organisational constraints that may affect your findings. Your recommendations may also suggest areas for further research.

Your thesis should be organised, well presented and researched and fully and accurately referenced. The literature you select should be relevant and significant. You should demonstrate an ability to précis and to compare and contrast views.

Drawing up the Research Proposal

- **Title**. This may change during the course of your research. Initially it should mirror your research question.

- **Background**. This should state why you think your research is necessary. Set out the research question and why it has aroused your curiosity.

- **Research question and objectives**. These should leave your tutor in no doubt what you are trying to achieve.

- **Method: research design and data collection**. This will show how you hope to go about your research. The research problem should dictate the research method. State where you are going to do your research and who the research population is going to be. State what research techniques you are going to adopt such as interviews, questionnaires, statistical methods, examination of company records or any combination of techniques. Issues of access and ethics should be addressed.

- **Timescale**. Build in buffer time, as research always takes longer than anticipated.

- **Resources needed**. Consider time, finance, data access and equipment.

- **References**. You should give a page or two of references. You must give the impression that your initial literature review has been reasonably thorough. The references must be directly relevant to your research question. Use the Harvard system of cross-referencing the text to the list of references. In the text, use the author's surname, the date of publication and the page numbers, if appropriate. In the list of references, give the author's full name, date of publication, title, place of publication and the name of the publisher.

A Research Timescale

This is an estimate of how long each stage of the process will take. It highlights the need to plan each stage of your work and have time deadlines for each stage. The following is based on a thesis where you have six months to complete the job and is suggested for guidance only:

- Research proposal to be completed and agreed with your tutor in month one;

- Initial literature review during month one;

- Research questions and objectives defined during month two;

- Draft literature review during month three;

- Design empirical research during month four;

- Implement empirical research during month four;

- Write up the empirical research and do the analysis during month five;

- First draft of thesis during month six;

- Submission of thesis at end of month six.

Thesis Layout

- **Abstract**.

- **List of contents**.

- **Introduction**. This should set out an outline of the research issue and why you thought that this was worth investigating. It should include your research question and research objectives. Put the work in the organisational context in which you carried out the empirical research. Give a brief indication of the conceptual framework adopted and an overview of the structure and content of the thesis.

- **Literature research**. Describe how you carried this out, what you researched and what you found. Categorise the information and show the case for and against the thesis.

- **Empirical research**. Discuss the model adopted and why you choose this model in preference to others. Indicate the reason why you rejected other models.

- **Main Body**. This should describe how you went about your study, the method of research adopted and what you found. This should include a comparison of the findings from your literature and empirical research. Do they support each other? If not, why not?

- **Conclusion**.

- **Bibliography**.

Preparation of Thesis

- WAYGO. Prepare an outline of your thesis early on. A good way of doing this is to prepare your list of contents, which is the map of your proposed thesis. The appendices, bibliography, and list of illustrations can be done in between other jobs. Multi-tasking is the approach to adopt.

- Use index cards to take notes as you do your research. Record full details of sources needed to compile your bibliography.

- Physical elements: you need a hard cover with title, a similar page inside, an abstract, list of contents, list of illustrations, main text, appendices, bibliography and references and a glossary if necessary. You should use the Harvard system of referencing for your bibliography and references.

- Illustrations. Use tables, charts, diagrams, models and maps as appropriate. Maps may be used to show the layout of factories, offices and so on. Make sure your illustrations add to your work rather than detract from it.

Writing the Abstract

The abstract, together with the findings, conclusions and recommendation section, is the most important part of your thesis. It is probably the only part that some people will read, so it is important that it gives an accurate representation of the main work. Generally, the abstract should be between one and two pages in length. It should be objective, precise and easy to read.

It is difficult to write a good abstract. Some people wait until the end of the thesis to write the abstract. An alternative and better approach is to write it at the start, as it gives you a brief overview of the thesis. You can always change it as you progress or at the end of the thesis. The abstract should stick exactly to what you have written in your thesis. The abstract is not the place for elaboration or adding in new ideas.

The abstract should answer the following:

- The research question;

- Its importance;

- The research methods used;

- Summary of findings, conclusions and recommendations.

Reports

As part of your job, you may be called upon to write reports. As part of degree programmes, you may be required to do written assignments or projects that are expected to follow the report format. The general approach is similar to that of writing a thesis, but not as rigorous. The ABCs of good report writing are accuracy, brevity, clarity and simplicity. Well-written reports follow the following structure:

- **Title page** should include the title, date, reference number, classification (confidential or otherwise), author's name, who commissioned the report and to whom the report is to be sent.

- **Management summary** should include the purpose and scope, method of investigation, findings, conclusions and recommendations.

- **Contents list**.

- **Introduction** should include the terms of reference, brief history of the topic, reasons for the report, who the report is for, limitations, treatment of the subject and special considerations.

- **Body** should include the method of investigation and the detailed findings.

- **Findings** should be itemised and categorised.

- **Conclusions** should be consistent, reasonable, clear, concise and itemised.

- **Recommendations** should be sound, well defined, concise, itemised, discreet and fully considered.

- **References** should include author, date, title of publication, place of publication and publisher.

- **Appendices** may include statistical tables, detailed results of surveys, graphs, summary of results from elsewhere, correspondence, quotations, maps, charts and diagrams.

- **Glossary** if there are a lot of technical terms and abbreviations in the report.

Effective Report Writing

Before you write:

- Plan your report in the form of a learning map.

- Be clear what your purpose is. What are you trying to achieve?

- Identify the information you want to get across.

- Bring together the resources, such as notes and references, that you need to do the writing.

During the writing:

- Avoid irrelevancy.

- Arrange your material in a logical sequence.

- Structure using sections, headings and numbered paragraphs.

- Make the layout and content user-friendly.

- As you write, keep the reader's needs in mind all the time.

- Be clear, direct and concise.

- Choose the right words for the job. Use concrete words rather than abstract words.

- Avoid repetition.
- Do a spellcheck.

After the writing:

- Check your work.
- Get a reliable colleague to read it for their honest opinion.

The more you practise report writing, the better you will become.

Order of Writing

This is really a matter of taste, but the following order for writing the report is often suggested:

- Body of report
- Findings
- Conclusions
- Recommendations
- Introduction
- Appendices
- Glossary
- Bibliography and references
- Management summary or abstract.

Checklist for a Better Thesis

The following points, which have been expanded and adapted from Hansen and Waterman (1966), will help you to evaluate your thesis before submission. When you are doing your thesis, tick each issue off as you address it:

The Research Question

- Did you clearly state and define the research problem?

- Did you formulate the research objectives?

- Is the problem important? Would the solution or partial solution of this problem make an important contribution to knowledge or practice; or has this same problem been researched a number of times before?

- Is the problem researchable? Are there plenty of books, articles and research papers available to support your thesis? What logical or practical limitations of the research should be considered?

- Have you set the boundaries for your problem? A thorough investigation of a narrow problem is better than a cursory examination of too broad a problem. Depth is more important than breadth. The more specific the area of your study the better.

- Have you identified and stated the limitations inherent in the study? Most studies are limited by one or more of the following: data-gathering techniques and instruments; sources of data; ability of the researcher; bias; and the money and time available to the researcher. Both the researcher and the reader should be aware of these limitations in interpreting the data.

- Did you test the hypothesis and answer the research questions?

- Did you describe the background or historical development of the problem?

- Have you clearly stated any assumptions made?

Logic and Sequence

- Have you used figures and models in the body of your thesis to illustrate and support points made?

- Have you relegated items such as details of procedures, questionnaires, estimates, maps, correspondence, diagrams and so on to the appendices?

- Have you numbered the appendices consecutively?

- Have you used organisers as appropriate, such as chapter headings, section headings, subheadings, paragraphs, bullet points, italics, bold for headings and so on?

- Have you numbered your pages? In the centre of the bottom margin is fine.

- Have you organised your thesis with an introduction, a body (research methodology — empirical and literature) and an end section giving the findings, conclusions and recommendations?

- Does your introduction state the key issues of the topic and set out the scope and limitations of the study?

- Is your thesis laid out in a logical sequence? Do conclusions and recommendations follow on logically from the findings?

- Does each of your paragraphs start with a topic sentence, which is developed in the rest of the paragraph?

- Have you illustrated your thesis with figures, diagrams, graphs, barcharts and models as appropriate?

- Does your thesis show evidence of insight, innovation and originality?

- Have you kept within the required length laid down by your examination body?

Use of Language

- Have you included a glossary of terms if your thesis contains a lot of technical words and abbreviations?

- Have you used the proper convention for quotations, such as short quotations within single quotation marks, double quotation marks for quotes within quotes. Quotations of more than 30 words should be indented.

- Is your grammar, spelling and punctuation of a high standard? Don't rely solely on your "spellchecker". Check through your thesis yourself as well.

- Where possible, have you kept your sentences short and clear?

- Have you avoided the use of clichés, slang, inappropriate jargon and verbosity?

- Have you used concrete words rather than abstract words where possible?

- Have you checked your script for tautology (saying the same thing twice in different words)?

- Check that your writing style is specific rather than general.

Literature Research

- Have you selected relevant and significant literature?

- Have you demonstrated an ability to précis and to compare and contrast views?

- Is your thesis fully and accurately referenced (e.g. Harvard) with a reference and bibliography included?

- Have you carried out a critical review of previous research?

- Have you shown the relationship between your current research and research that was done previously?

- Did your review include research of the literature in related disciplines that might have implications for the present study?

- Does your literature research show evidence of wide reading?

Empirical Research

- Did you select appropriate research methods, having regard to the particular constraints of the situation and your own capabilities?

- Did you describe the research methods completely and clearly? If so, another competent investigator should be able to repeat the study without difficulty.

- Have you followed good design practice when drawing up your questionnaire? You should consult a book on questionnaire design or study a well-laid-out questionnaire.

- Have you carefully worded the questions and made sure they are relevant to your research requirements?

- Did you identify the sample population?

- Was the sampling method clear, appropriate and comprehensive?

- Were all variables that might influence the study recognised and controlled by the research design? Were the limitations, if any, acknowledged and discussed?

- Did you use valid and reliable methods to collect the data? Were you careful to avoid bias?

- Were you careful and accurate in recording and summarising the data?

- Did you use and apply correctly appropriate statistical or other methods to analyse the data?

- Did you defend the methods you have chosen and give reasons for rejecting alternative methods?

- Did you demonstrate an ability to carry out the chosen methods effectively?

- Did you reflect, with hindsight, on the advantages and disadvantages of the chosen methods?

Findings, Conclusions and Recommendations

- Did you relate your empirical findings to the literature review and theoretical concepts?

- Did you identify the organisational constraints affecting your findings?

- Did you demonstrate an understanding of the significance of the findings?

- Are your findings and conclusions supported by and in harmony with the body of the thesis?

- Were the findings compared with findings of similar studies reported in the review of the literature?

- Are your findings and conclusions free of bias?

- Did you make recommendations for further research? No one has worked as closely as you with the topic and you may see opportunities for further research.

- Did you highlight the implications of the study for practice and in particular for your own firm?

- Are your findings, conclusions and recommendations carefully organised, categorised, well presented and properly referenced?

Presentation

- Is your thesis attractively bound with proper headings?

- Is the title clear, complete and concise? Does it show your name, degree sought, and date?

- Have you included a title page flyer inside the cover?

- Have you used the recommended spacing? Double-spacing or one-and-half lines is the usual.

- Have you left margins at the top, bottom, left and right? Make sure the margin on the left leaves sufficient room for binding.

- Have you used A4 paper and typed on one side only or other college requirements?

- Have you included a thesis abstract?

- Is the abstract a clear statement and summary of the important parts of the study?

- Have you included a table of contents?

- Have you included a list of exhibits? Have you used a numbering system for the content of your thesis?

Finally . . .

- Did you back up your work on a floppy disk?

- Did you get a reliable third party to read your thesis before you finalised it?

- Did you keep in touch with your tutor throughout the process?

Summary

The six Cs of good writing are:

- Clear

- Concise

- Complete

- Concrete

- Correct

- Coherent.

A suggested model for a thesis is:

- Define the research model

- Review the literature

- Formulate a hypothesis

- Two aspects to research design: the literature and empirical research

- Implement

- Interpret

- Report.

Generally, examiners want:

- Abstract

- Introduction

- Body

- Findings, conclusions and recommendations.

A suggested approach to the preparation of a thesis:

- WAYGO, which means write as you go
- Decide on illustrations
- Use index cards for note-taking
- Know the physical elements required by your college.

A suggested structure for reports and assignments is:

- Title page
- Management summary
- Contents list
- Introduction
- Body
- Findings
- Conclusions
- Recommendations
- References
- Appendices
- Glossary.

A detailed checklist for the preparation of a thesis was given in the chapter.

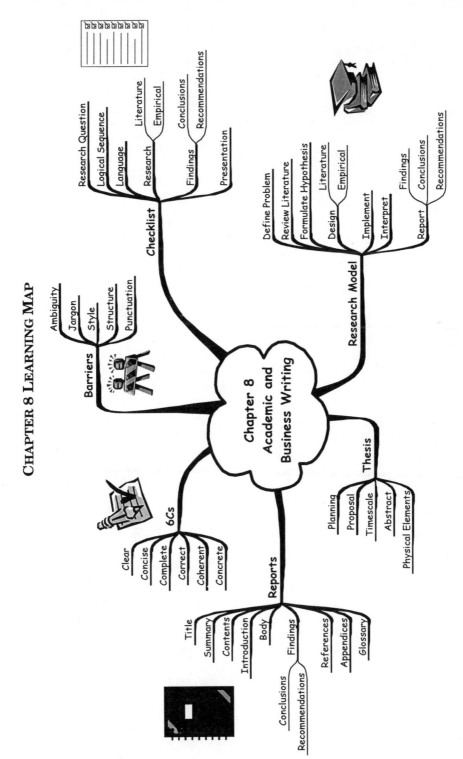

CHAPTER 8 LEARNING MAP

Chapter 8
Academic and
Business Writing

Checklist
- Research Question
- Logical Sequence
- Language
- Research
  - Literature
  - Empirical
- Findings
  - Conclusions
  - Recommendations
- Presentation

Barriers
- Ambiguity
- Jargon
- Style
- Structure
- Punctuation

Research Model
- Define Problem
- Review Literature
- Formulate Hypothesis
- Design
  - Literature
  - Empirical
- Implement
- Interpret
  - Findings
  - Conclusions
  - Recommendations
- Report

6Cs
- Clear
- Concise
- Complete
- Correct
- Coherent
- Concrete

Reports
- Title
- Summary
- Contents
- Introduction
- Body
- Findings
  - Conclusions
  - Recommendations
- References
- Appendices
- Glossary

Thesis
- Planning
- Proposal
- Timescale
- Abstract
- Physical Elements

9

Examination Techniques

"Backward, turn backward, O Time, in your flight,
And tell me just one thing I studied last night."
— Hobart Brown

- ◆ *What is the PASSED model?*

- ◆ *What do examiners want?*

- ◆ *What is the RTQPARM model?*

- ◆ *How do I do multiple choice questions?*

- ◆ *How do I prepare and write case studies?*

As part of your career development, you are likely to pursue further studies. You have probably gone rusty on examination technique, so now might be a good time to brush up on the essentials. The key to exam success can be summed up by the four Ps: Plan, Prepare, Practice and Presentation.

The PASSED Model

This is a mnemonic which stands for:

- **P**reparation

- **A**bsorb key points

- **S**uccess factors

- **S**ystematic approach

- **E**xaminers are human

- **D**ay of examination.

This mnemonic is elaborated on in the following sections.

Preparation

- Have a proper **revision timetable**. A timetable will focus your mind on what needs to be done. Remember, revision should have been an ongoing part of your study plan during the year. It is not always a good idea to miss lectures towards the end of a course in order to spend more time in revision. These last lectures may prove to be very useful. The lecturer may emphasise important points, draw conclusions and give hints on exam technique. For college exams, the lecturer may even provide some clues as to what is likely to come up!

- **Space your revision**. Study for time blocks of one hour, with rest and review periods in between. A short walk or some push-ups, stretches, or other simple physical exercises will keep your body fit and your mind alert.

- **Variety**. Don't study the same topic all night. Study the most difficult subject first, when you are the most mentally alert. Alternate subjects to maintain interest and freshness of mind. Also, alternate approaches such as reading, reviewing, and doing problems. Always remember the "say and do" principle. Research shows that we remember only 10 per cent of what we read, 20 per cent of what we see, but 90 per cent of what we say and do. So, whenever possible, read, review and do.

- **Planning**. Practise budgeting your time and planning your answers under mock examination conditions. Give yourself difficult practice exams with problems that you never saw before. Check your attempts against model answers. If you can get 100 per cent in these tests, you are more likely to do very well in the exam.

- **Trend analysis**. Forewarned is forearmed. Study past examinations for topical issues and for areas of the course that are of particular concern to the examiner. However, ideally it is best to master all aspects of the course so that if your favourite topics do not come up, it won't matter too much. If you are attending college, lecturers may occasionally point out topics that are particularly important or, conversely, topics that will not be examined.

- Do an **error analysis** of your typical errors. Look over any classwork, previous exams or feedback from lecturers to see where you typically go wrong. Take a mental note of these errors and make sure that you will not repeat them in the future.

- **Mental rehearsal**. Psychologists maintain that mental rehearsal is nearly as good as the actual examination process. Visualise yourself in the examination room and rehearse the process you are likely to go through on examination day. See yourself as calm, relaxed, alert and confident in the exam room. See yourself correctly answering all the questions and the exam going extremely well for you. Do this visualisation each day in the days preceding the exam. Do it again just before you enter the exam room. Use positive affirmations to programme your mind for success. Say to yourself: "I am confident and alert when doing exams"; "I'm a very good student"; "I successfully complete exams". Combine your visualisation with relaxation techniques such as breathing exercises or meditation.

- **Anticipation**. Check out the location of the examination centre. Reconnoitre and time how long it takes to get to the centre. Anticipate traffic patterns on particular days. Allow yourself plenty of time to get there.

- Make sure to **get enough sleep** in the days before the exam.

Absorb Key Facts

- **Learning maps and cue cards**. Do not attempt to learn new material at this stage, unless it is something important that you have overlooked. Ideally, you will have prepared learning map summaries and cue cards for key areas of your course.

- **Examination paper structure**. Study the structure of past examinations. How many questions are you required to answer? Out of how many? Are there compulsory questions on the paper? Check the length of the paper and calculate how long you should spend on each question. All of this information will help you put a strategy in place for the exam day. Have up to ten past examination papers for each of your subjects and revise from the answers. For some subjects that change frequently, such as information technology, it may not be appropriate to go back for more than a few years.

Success Factors

- **Time management**. One of the main reasons people fail examinations is that they run out of time. Time management is just as important in the examination room as it is in other areas of your life. Allocate time to each question in proportion to the marks allowed. For a three-hour paper, this works out at 1.8 minutes per mark. So for a question with 30 marks, you should allocate 54 minutes (1.8 x 30). Five minutes of this time should be reserved for planning and a few minutes should be set aside for review. Spend approximately 45 minutes actually doing the question. Apply this approach to each question. Reserve a few minutes at the end of your examination to quickly review the entire script. Only add things at the end if, as you read, you see that important conclusions are missing. If you run out of time and there is still one question unanswered, you could very well get some marks by outlining briefly how you would have answered the question. When you have spent this time allocation, move on to the next question.

- **Law of diminishing returns**. A law of diminishing returns operates in relation to examination questions. The first few marks on a question are relatively easy to get, whereas the last few are extremely difficult to earn. Thus, it is easier to score a few marks on a question which at first sight you thought you knew little about. This is better than spending more time on a question that you know a lot about and have already done justice to.

- **Balanced answers**. You should write approximately the same length of answer to questions carrying equal marks. For example, writing four pages of script for one question as against one for another shows either poor time management or a detailed knowledge of one topic and a superficial knowledge of another. Similarly, an unbalanced answer in which some sections receive too much attention shows a lack of planning or judgement and an inefficient use of time.

- **Write something**. If you write nothing, you cannot gain marks. Candidates who write something relevant will usually gain some marks. These marks could turn a borderline fail into a pass. Go into the examination determined to succeed. So give every question your best shot, even if you feel you know very little about the topic.

- **Breadth of knowledge**. Remember that examiners are generally looking for a breadth of knowledge over the whole syllabus, not depth of knowledge in a narrow field. So spending too much time on a favoured topic at the expense of others may cost you a pass. Time is also wasted copying rough answers and then recopying them. Also, some candidates have a tendency to rewrite the question, which is more time wasted.

- **Relevance**. This is probably the most prevalent reason why people fail examinations. They probably haven't read the question properly or they are just having a go. In any event, you are unlikely to get any marks for an answer that does not address the issues in the question. Every examiner complains about answers from students who have anticipated a particular question and memorised a full answer to it. They then proceed to write out the memorised answer in full, regardless of whether the answer addresses the question. Such attempts get very few marks or even none at all. As you write your answer, stop occasionally and check that it is consistently relevant to the question asked and that you are not straying away from the point.

- **Presentation**. Use headings, subheadings, listing of points and so on as appropriate. Drop a line between each paragraph. The first sentence in your paragraph should be the topic sentence. The rest of the paragraph should expand and illustrate the main idea. Each paragraph should be built around one idea.

- **Preparation**. Many people present themselves for examination completely unprepared. Your performance in examinations is directly correlated with the amount of time, application and effort put in. If you follow my advice on time management, your study time will be both productive and effective.

- **Giving the examiner what they want**. Examiners want scripts that are well laid out, readable, relevant and tidy. They also want you to follow any exam instructions given.

Systematic Approach

Before you begin, write down the start and finish time of each question and then make sure to stick to it. Then apply the RTQPARM technique, which is a systematic approach to answering examination questions. It stands for: **R**ead, **T**hink, **Q**uestion, **P**lan, **A**nswer, **R**eview and **M**ove on.

- **Read the question**. Concentrate on what you are required to do first, as indicated at the end of the question. Then read the entire question a few times until you have the gist of what is required. Note any special requirements, indicated by words such as *list*, *detail*, *advise*, *explain*, *report* and so on. When asked to list or outline, do not write an essay. When asked to summarise, do not give examples. When asked to report on, a report format is required. Failure to follow examination instructions will lose you marks.

- **Think about the question**. Think and reflect on the issues raised for a few moments. "Stop and think" should be your motto.

- **Question the question**. Get behind the requirements of the question by asking the following questions: What does the examiner want? What is the subject area generally concerned with? What are the fundamental issues behind the question? What are the facts pertinent to the issues raised? How can I present them in a clear, concise, coherent, lucid and logical fashion?

- **Plan your answer**. Draw a learning map of the key points to answer the question. Ask yourself again if these points are truly relevant to the question asked.

- **Answer the question**. Use the key points of your plan as captions and write paragraphs around each. Stop after every few paragraphs and recheck that you are being consistently relevant and are not straying from the point. Use a deductive approach (make an inference from general theories to the particular problem posed). This is in preference to an inductive approach (where students try to draw general conclusions from specific examples or, indeed, personal views). Remember, examinations are tests of theoretical knowledge. Theory may be illustrated by practical relevant experience. This is recommended, as it shows that you can relate theory to practice. However, inventing your own theories, which is what you are actually doing by drawing inferences from your own practical experiences or personal views, is not acceptable to examiners. The examiner requires evidence in the form of well-balanced arguments supported by reference to authors, books, articles, research studies and also radio and television documentaries.

- **Review**. Quickly review your answer, picking up misspellings, incomplete or nonsensical statements, lack of conclusions and so on. Apply logic to calculations. Check that they are within the parameters of the "ball park" figures, which you should have precalculated on a common-sense basis for comparison as to reasonableness. This applies particularly to costing and management accounting answers.

- **Move on to the next question**. Move on to the next question and start the RTQPARM approach again.

During the examination, practise saying positive affirmations to yourself. These will keep your mind focused away from distracting or disturbing thoughts and help you maintain a positive attitude. Say some of the following affirmations to yourself:

- *I am a brilliant student.*

- *I am capable and doing very well in this exam.*

- *I am supremely confident.*

- *My mind is clear, sharp and alert.*

- *I am an intelligent and talented person.*

- *I am relaxed, calm and confident.*

- *I am a good time manager.*

Examiners are Human

Examiners are not ogres. They want you to pass the examination, but not at the expense of diluting standards. They have taken many examinations themselves so they do empathise with you. However, do not write notes pleading to the examiner for leniency. This is both irritating to the examiner, immature on your part and a waste of time.

Just like you, they get annoyed, irritated and bored. Marking papers can be a tedious job at the best of times. The examiner tries to mark them in a conscientious, fair and honourable fashion. To keep the examiner satisfied, interested and favourably disposed toward you, you should at least follow the examination instructions, and write legibly. If the examiner can't read what you have written, then he or she can't award the appropriate marks.

Examiners know their subject, they can't be bluffed and they understand English. They are not interested in your pet theories, prejudices, religious beliefs, political opinions, moral judgements, social comment, biases, hatreds and so on. All they want is pertinent knowledge, facts and theory related to the question set. They take the most rational, sensible and logical interpretation of the questions set and mark accordingly. Great care is taken in formulating questions and they are checked and rechecked to ensure clarity and precision of words.

To pass, you must reach the required standard in each paper. Some professional examination bodies publish explanation grades and band of marks, which are well worth consulting.

Day of the Examination

In the examination room, when you receive the paper, make sure that you read it from beginning to end. Before this, provided you have the opportunity while the invigilator is handing out the papers, write in your examination number on as many of the sheets of stationery provided as possible. This saves vital minutes later on and gets you a little bit organised for the task ahead.

Read the instructions to candidates carefully. Decide what each question requires. Organise the order of the answers. Answer your "best" question first, making sure you do not spend too long on it in relation to the marks available. Then do your "second-best" question and so on. Remember, you need not answer the questions in the numerical sequence given on the question paper itself. However, when finished, you must put them in numerical sequence before you hand them in.

Your examination paper may contain a mix of long and short questions. Don't fall into the trap of assuming that length correlates with difficulty and thus avoid doing the long questions. In fact, the converse is often true.

Multiple-choice Questions

Objective testing is now a popular form of examination. Answers are either right or wrong. Multiple-choice questions are the most popular form of objective test. In a multiple-choice examination, the candidate is required to select the correct or best response from several options. Items consist of a stem in the form of an incomplete statement, diagram, calculation or task to be solved. You must pick the correct response from the options given. The incorrect responses are called distracters.

There are two basic kinds of multiple-choice questions. In one, an incomplete statement can be combined with various options to make a complete statement, which is either true or false. In the other, a question is followed by various statements, one of which must be chosen as the correct answer.

The following approach to answering multiple-choice questions is suggested:

1. Read and heed the instructions. How much time is allowed? How exactly are you told to complete the answers? The latter is essential if the tests are computer-scored.

2. Work through the whole paper. Answer those you find easy now. You can return to the more difficult questions later. Mark these on the margin with a question mark.

3. Highlight key words to ensure that you read and understand them fully.

4. Pick your best alternative; that is, the one you feel is nearest the correct answer. Eliminate those you feel are incorrect. This will limit your choice and at the same time increase your chance of getting the right answer.

5. Don't procrastinate. You need to get through the test within the time constraints set. Time management is, therefore, of the utmost importance.

6. Return to the more difficult questions. On rereading, the answers may come to mind. Where you don't know the answer, use logic and common sense. Random guesses are seldom correct.

7. Most people can recognise more facts than they can recall. As a result, most students perform better on multiple-choice tests than on other tests.

8. Remember that on multiple-choice exams, your first response is often your best. So don't change your answer unless you are very confident that you are incorrect. Many students change correct answers for incorrect ones.

Case Studies — The IDEAS Model

Case studies are now a part of most business degree and professional qualification courses. All or part of an examination paper may be devoted to a case study. The following approach to solving case studies is worth adopting. First, read through the case study quickly to familiarise yourself with the case. Then read it in detail, applying the systematic approach to case studies as suggested in the IDEAS model, which is illustrated in the following diagram:

CASE STUDIES: IDEAS MODEL

Identify the Problem
Describe the Facts
Examine the Facts
Alternatives Explored
Select Best Alternative

Identify the Problem

Identify the problem, or problems, and the issues involved. Identify the *real* problem. Einstein wrote:

> The formulation of a problem is far more essential than its solution, which may be merely a matter of mathematical or experimental skill. To raise new questions, new possibilities, to regard old problems from a new angle, requires creative imagination.

Do not confuse the symptoms with the problem. For example, an influenza virus causes a headache, sore throat, sneezing, tiredness, perspiration and aching joints. These are symptoms — the action of the virus is the problem. However, identifying the symptoms may help you to identify the problem.

What is a problem? In very simple terms, it is the difference or gap between an actual situation and some desired state. In management, this is called gap analysis, the gap being the difference between the existing or extrapolated position and the objectives. The gap is filled by the implementation of appropriate strategies.

Problems in a business situation are usually interlinked and interact and affect each other in a complex, multifaceted manner. For example, many case studies are usually written around specific issues. The examiner normally sets out the problem for solution in the questioning approach: What is the problem or problems? Where does it occur? When does it occur? Whose problem is it? Why does the problem occur? What are the reasons for the problem? How can the problem be overcome?

In management, problems may be caused at corporate, functional or line level, inter alia, by poor performance or standards in planning, leadership, motivation, control, communication, coordination, setting objectives, time management, delegation, interpersonal relationships, interdepartmental conflicts, organisational politics, inadequate training, discipline and many more. Remember that a problem well stated is halfway to being solved.

Describe the Facts

Record and summarise the facts given. Focus on the facts appropriate to the solution of the questions asked. More importantly, identify the facts that are *not* given but that in practice would need to be taken into account for a good decision. Why do case study writers leave out information or give incomplete information? There are four possibilities:

1. The information may have been unobtainable.

2. It was left out deliberately because its omission made for a better and more focused case study. Logistical information may have been excluded because the case writer wished students to concentrate on the strategic and organisational aspects of the case. Production and human resource management information may have been excluded because the case writer wanted to focus the examinee's attention on the marketing issues.

3. In some examinations, case studies must be kept to a reasonable length because of the time constraint. Information, there-

fore, is not included because of the need to keep the case study short. This would suggest that only essential information be given, peripheral information being excluded. Therefore, missing information may have to be assumed or extrapolated by the student.

4. Students sometimes think that because certain information is not provided, it is irrelevant. This is not a wise assumption. The examiner may be trying to see if you can draw on your knowledge and experience to fill in the gaps.

If faced with a similar problem in a work situation, how would you solve it? This will force you to consider the practical implications and constraints associated with the problem. Where figures are provided, they may also be incomplete.

Examine the Facts

Some analysis, classification, reclassification and interpretation of the facts may be appropriate and necessary to help you arrive at worthwhile decisions. When case studies are complex, it is difficult to keep all aspects of the problem in mind at once. The span of attention is only between five and nine items. You should, therefore, group data to keep it within your attention span. Use learning maps, tables, graphs, algorithms, diagrams and flowcharts as appropriate for this.

Apply problem-solving techniques, where applicable, such as ratio analysis, decision trees, cause and effect analysis, force field analysis, Pareto analysis, discounted cash flow, marginal costing, break even analysis, gap analysis, growth share matrix, SWOT analysis, the product life cycle and so on. Display to the examiner that you can integrate and apply the concepts, knowledge and theory from your course of studies to the practical requirements of the case study.

Alternatives Explored

This is the creative stage of the problem-solving sequence. One source of inspiration should be your own experience. This may come from your own work experience in an organisation, your leisure time experience of being a member of a voluntary or professional organisation or your everyday experience of dealing with other organisations as a customer. How would these organisations solve the problem? Novel solutions, provided they are sensible, acceptable and practical, may also win you good marks. Brainstorming and lateral thinking are well-known methods for coming up with original ideas. Use a learning map to get your ideas down on paper and to show the interrelationships between different ideas.

In the specialised areas of management, there are well-known, tried-and-tested standard procedures, techniques and models for helping to solve organisational problems.

Select Best Alternative

Having considered the alternative strategies that the company should pursue, pick the best alternative. Obviously, there are many alternative solutions to any problem. Therefore, you should rank alternatives in terms of their benefits. Look at the pros and cons of each. Eliminate the impractical and less profitable. Risk and uncertainty should also be taken into account. Qualitative outcomes of solutions should be considered.

The criteria for the best alternative should include cost–benefit analysis, practicability and acceptability of the proposed solution to the case study under examination. What is the effect on the bottom-line result? To be worthwhile, the overall profitability, effectiveness and efficiency of the organisation should improve.

Describe how you would implement the solution in practice; for example, via delegation, training and development, improved communication, counselling and reorganisation. List the type of problems, constraints and obstacles that may be encountered and have to be overcome in practice when an attempt is made to sell and implement the solution. For example, limited resources of staff and time, staff resistance to change, trade union objections, company policy and so on. When will implementation take place? How will it be done? Who will do it? How much will it cost?

What will be the likely corporate, financial, production, personnel, marketing, organisational, behavioural, customer and competitive implications of implementing the change? What contingency plans should you make to overcome likely problems? Describe how you would monitor and follow up to ensure that the suggested change was implemented correctly. Remember that management of time is just as important when answering case studies as when answering more conventional examination questions.

Case Studies — What Examiners Want

The following are the three main faults by students when answering case studies in examinations:

1. Wasting time by restating the information given in the question.

2. Failing to draw conclusions and recommendations that follow logically from the information provided.

3. Making totally unjustified assumptions about the situation described. This in turn is likely to lead to quite irrelevant answers.

Reports

Many examinations require answers in the form of reports. Examiners often complain that when students are required to answer in the form of reports, they write an essay. You will lose valuable marks if you do not comply with examination requirements. Reports are a very important aspect of everyday business life and examiners expect that you are able to write them. Reports are discussed in Chapter 8 and you should go back to this and review the systematic approach to report writing.

Summary

The PASSED model will help you remember the key ingredients for success in examinations. This stands for:

- **P**reparation
- **A**bsorb
- **S**uccess factors

- **S**ystematic approach
- **E**xaminers are human
- **D**ay of examination.

Use a systematic approach to answering examination questions:
- **R**ead the question carefully
- **T**hink about the question
- **Q**uestion the question
- **P**lan your answer
- **A**nswer the question
- **R**eview your answer
- **M**ove on to the next question.

The IDEAS model for solving case studies is:
- **I**dentify the problem
- **D**escribe the facts
- **E**xamine the facts
- **A**lternatives explored
- **S**elect best alternative, implement and check.

A suggested approach to answering multiple-choice questions was given. The importance of report writing in examinations was highlighted.

CHAPTER 9 LEARNING MAP

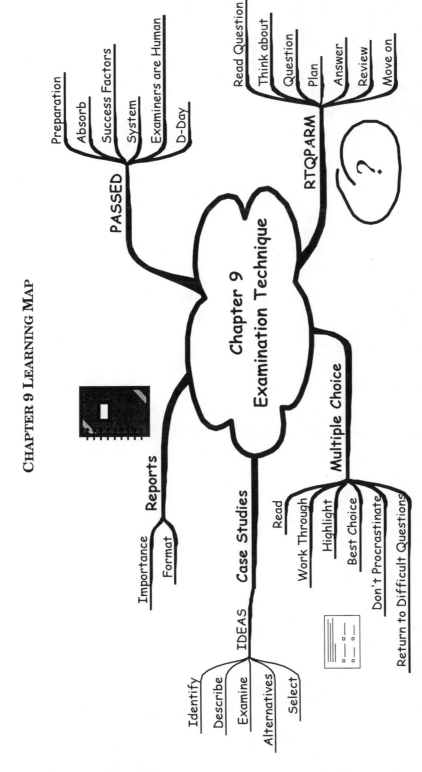

Chapter 9
Examination Technique

PASSED
- Preparation
- Absorb
- Success Factors
- System
- Examiners are Human
- D-Day

RTQPARM
- Read Question
- Think about Question
- Plan
- Answer
- Review
- Move on

Reports
- Importance
- Format

Case Studies

IDEAS
- Identify
- Describe
- Examine
- Alternatives
- Select

Multiple Choice
- Read
- Work Through
- Highlight
- Best Choice
- Don't Procrastinate
- Return to Difficult Questions

On-the-Job Learning

"Personally I'm always ready to learn, although I do not always like being taught." — Winston Churchill

---

♦ *What does LAYGO mean?*

♦ *What are the techniques of on-the-job learning?*

♦ *What are the CRAMP and KASH models?*

♦ *What are the basic managerial competencies?*

LAYGO — Learn As You Go

On-the-job learning is the greatest source of learning for a manager. Burgoyne (1999) found that 80 per cent of the skills developed by managers were got from on-the-job learning experiences. This contrasts with 20 per cent for formal training and development activities.

The Principle of Reciprocity suggests that in developing other people, you are also developing yourself. Learning is a two-way process. You are the only person who can take responsibility for your learning and development. The following are some approaches:

- **Self-directed learning**. Take responsibility for your own learning.

- **Self-reflection**. Adopt a reflective approach to learning. Follow the learning cycle of "do something, think about it, conclude and do something differently".

- **Learn from your mistakes**. Somebody once said that inside every mistake there are lessons waiting to get out. Learning from experience is the most important of all the life skills. We learn well and fast when we experience the consequences of what we do — and don't do.

- **Continuous improvement**. You should not be satisfied with your current level of expertise but should try to improve all the time.

- **Career development**. Seek out opportunities that will stretch your capabilities.

- **Action learning**. You learn by doing things and reflecting on how you performed. The great achievers in life do things rather than talk about them.

- **Just-in-time learning**. Develop your own just-in-time learning resources. Buy encyclopaedias on CD-ROM and install them on your computer. This provides you with knowledge at your fingertips. Use the Internet to explore developments in your area of interest. On your desktop computer at work, build in learning resources such as job aids, expert systems and management information systems to help you do your job more effectively. Use e-mail to keep in touch with your colleagues and share your learning experiences.

Managers report that the most significant learning experiences of their development have been on-the-job experiences. It is very difficult if not impossible to replicate the type of learning experience you get on-the-job on a formal management development programme. There are numerous approaches to on-the-job training that will help you in your quest for development. The following are some of the best known.

On-the-Job Learning: Groups

- **Projects or task force**. These can range from a few days' duration to a few months'. This may involve the computerisation of a manual system, introducing new equipment, the relocation of offices or improving some aspect of the business. Projects have a sponsor and should be guided by written terms of reference. They are normally conducted by teams and operate to deadlines. A formal report is issued at the end of the project, making recommendations. Projects provide many learning opportunities, including developing interpersonal relationship skills, learning how to co-operate in a team situation, working to a deadline, coping with unusual situations, developing report-writing skills, and gaining experience in an area where you would not normally work. Projects often provide an opportunity to work across a wide range of functions. Some project teams are responsible for implementation as well as making recommendations. This type of project provides the strongest form of development. Project teams are often set up to manage change including acquisitions, mergers and divestments. The manager involved should be debriefed during and at the end of the project to see what learning opportunities have occurred and how they have contributed to the manager's development.

- **Committee work**. Committees are formal groups with a chairperson, secretary, an agenda and rules of conduct. Some committees are ongoing, such as safety committees and suggestion scheme committees. Other committees may be set up for a particular purpose, such as a committee set up to investigate customer complaints or a judicial enquiry. Committee work is a great developmental opportunity for a manager. The manager will learn how committees are organised, administered and run; about agendas and minutes of meetings; how to operate in a group and co-operate with other people, sometimes from different departments and different disciplines; about the unique perspectives of functional managers and how to work with different levels of managers; and how to manage meetings and influence people. Committee work also provides a very good insight into human behaviour.

- **Meetings** are another opportunity for a manager to develop a whole range of interpersonal and organisational skills, depending on the role the manager has at the meeting. The manager can find out how to chair a meeting, how to draw up an agenda, and how to keep minutes. He or she can become a student of human nature by studying how people interact at meetings and observing body language in action. Meetings are also a great way of networking, getting to know what other managers do and developing contacts throughout the organisation.

On-the-Job Learning: Personal Development

- **Job rotation**. This gives managers a series of lateral job assignments in different parts of the organisation for a period of time from three months to twelve months. A switch between a line job and a functional job is particularly insightful. Here the manager learns the difference between the hands-on action-oriented approach required in a line job in compared to the more laid back and reflective style necessary in a staff role. The primary objective of job rotation is to improve managers' problem-solving and decision-making skills while at the same time giving them an overall perspective of the company and the interface between departments. Job rotation helps managers crystallise their career paths and improves job satisfaction and motivation. To maximise the effectiveness of job rotation, managers should be given the appropriate level of responsibility to use new skills and make decisions. Ideally, the job rotation programme should be supported by mentors who are available for coaching, counselling and advice. Role rotation within teams also provides opportunities for learning, as people struggle to master an unfamiliar role. On a more limited scale, task rotation within a section can provide wider experience and developmental opportunities.

- **Social occasions** develop interpersonal relationship skills. These may be occasions like the annual Christmas party, making presentations to staff who have been promoted or are leaving to take up opportunities elsewhere. Other occasions might be making presentations to staff on marriage, or making awards to staff for exceptional on-the-job performance or excellence in passing examinations. All of these opportunities give you a public profile and develop your interpersonal relationship skills as well as giving you practice at speaking in public.

- **Tasks**. These may be tasks delegated to you by your own manager. Routine tasks for the manager may very well provide a challenge to you because you have never done them before. You should let your manager know that you are eager to broaden your experience and take on extra responsibilities. These will give you an opportunity to show how good you are at taking on new challenges. This will show that you are not afraid of hard work and may help you become noticed in the organisation.

On-the-Job Learning: Benchmarking

- **Modelling**. Model yourself on successful business people or managers that you admire in your workplace, or indeed outside the workplace. Adopt the behaviours of your chosen role models. Learning from observation is a natural process. Children learn by watching their parents and other adults.

- **Visits** to customers, suppliers, competitors and other parts of your own company. These may be used to broaden a manager's experience. For example, a production manager may accompany a sales manager to see how sales are achieved and concluded and how customers are kept satisfied. This will give the production manager a unique insight into what marketing and sales are all about. Similarly, a production manager might be appointed to a working party on investment appraisal of a proposed factory extension. Here he or she will learn how accountants evaluate capital investment proposals using discounted cash flow techniques. Visits can also be used as a basis for benchmarking your systems, procedures and processes against those companies that you visit. These visits should demonstrate to you that there are different ways of doing things and different approaches to solving problems. Even in different parts of your own organisation, you often find new and novel ways of solving everyday problems and managing. If you send a member of your staff, you should debrief them on what they have learned when they come back.

- **Work shadowing**. This is where you observe someone else doing their job during a specific activity or period of time. Shadowing gives you the opportunity to observe the job of a senior manager at first hand. You observe the manager while negotiating, handling complaints, compiling budgets, answering correspondence, answering the phone, attending meetings, interviewing staff and drafting reports. You should pick up new ideas, insights, tips and techniques on how to be more efficient and effective in your job. You will also learn that different managers do things differently and have different types of leadership and communication styles. You will also learn that there are some things that you do better than your manager!

On-The-Job Learning: Demanding Work

- **Deputising** for your manager while he or she is on leave or away on business. This can be a great source of development, as you take on the full responsibilities of the manager while they are away. It is important that the manager lets everybody know that you have full authority in his absence. The longer the period the manager is away, the more developmental the opportunity. Although you might be "thrown in at the deep end", it is surprising how you will meet the challenge. You should view the situation as a great opportunity to learn a whole range of issues which a manager is confronted with on a day-to-day basis. Keep a learning log, as this will help you reflect on your learning experiences and inform the debriefing discussion on the manager's return.

- **Promotion**. When you are promoted, everything is new and therefore you go through an initial stage of continuous learning and challenge. In order to survive, you will have to learn very quickly to develop basic competencies in your new job. Don't be afraid to consult your staff as part of your team. You are not the sole repository of knowledge and experience. You have to go outside your comfort zone and use your initiative in situations that you are not used to. As well as the job challenges and more responsibility, you may have to form new relationships and network in a different circle. Promotion provides the best management development opportunity. Research has found that managers go through various stages when they move into a new job: taking hold; immersion; reshaping; consolidation; and refinement (see Mumford, 1997). The "taking hold" stage takes some time and during this stage the manager will need support.

- **Job enrichment and job enlargement**. Job enrichment is the process of giving a manager more responsible and demanding tasks to do. Job enlargement is giving a manager a greater variety of tasks to do. Both approaches can increase job satisfaction and motivation. Both, especially job enrichment, provide opportunities for learning and development. Job enrichment provides more opportunities for achievement, recognition, esteem and responsibility.

- **Budgeting**. Unless you are the departmental manager, you may not be responsible for drawing up the budget for your department. Budgeting is a great developmental opportunity and so make sure you get involved with your manager in the process. You will learn how to convert action programmes into money terms. You will learn how to formulate financial objectives, make forecasts, liaise with the finance department, negotiate and prioritise your budgetary resources, and control actual expenditure against budgets. In the process, you will get a great insight into the budgeting and financial reporting systems in the company. Being involved in the budgeting process is a great way of getting noticed in the company. However, beware, as in many organisations, reputations are made or broken depending on budgeting skills.

On-The-Job Learning: Communication Skills

- **Briefing**. This is the process of keeping staff up-to-date about events in the company. Staff are particularly interested in information that has a direct bearing on their jobs. This is a great opportunity for managers to practise their interpersonal relationship, presentation and communication skills. Briefing is a two way process: you brief your staff and they brief you. Listening, asking questions, interpreting and giving and receiving feedback are some of the skills you will develop. Briefings should be both frequent and regular. A cascading system, where one level of management briefs the next, is used in some companies.

- **Debriefing**. This is a great way of getting feedback from your staff. You should run debriefing sessions when staff return from formal training programmes or when they have finished major tasks or projects. Before the programme, you should brief staff on learning expectations. Debriefing is a great opportunity for you to ask probing questions and to determine what lessons your staff have learned from their experiences. Debriefing helps you keep in touch with what is happening within your area of responsibility. Debriefing will help your staff learn and develop. It also provides you with an opportunity to develop your communication skills by asking open-ended questions and probing for specific information.

- **Negotiation**. Negotiating is a process that tries to reach agreement between two or more different starting positions. Negotiations might be with large customers, suppliers, staff representatives or trade unions. Negotiations have various possible outcomes, such as win–win, win–lose, lose–lose and so on. From a learning point of view, the skills required to achieve a win–win solution are considerable and therefore stretch you more. You should attend a formal negotiation course to get the basic skills. You will learn about tactics and behaviour. You will learn a particular approach to communication — how to ask clarification questions, listen and summarise. You will learn how to be creative and how to disagree constructively.

- **Interviewing**. Interviews are a structured way to elicit as much information as possible from someone in a defined period of time. Volunteer to sit in on selection interviews in order to develop interviewing skills. You should attend a formal training programme in interviewing skills before you sit on an interview panel. You will learn how to ask open questions and how to put people at their ease. You will learn how to match up a person's qualifications, experience and personality with the requirements of the job. You will also use the skills developed when interviewing customers, suppliers and prospective management consultants.

- **Appraisal**. This is an interview to let staff know how they are getting along on the job. The review will investigate the staff's strengths and weaknesses, the reason behind successes and failures and how the employee can improve in the future. Goals for future performance are jointly agreed for review at the next appraisal interview and training and development needs identified. Appraisal interviews are usually held half-yearly or yearly, but mini-appraisals should be an ongoing feature of the job. If you are serious about the development of your staff, you will be a frequent appraiser. There are two great learning opportunities here for managers: first, as an appraiser of their own staff, and second, as an appraisee of their senior managers. As an appraiser, you will learn how to give feedback in the form of both praise and constructive criticism. You will also learn how to identify training needs to help the appraisee perform better in the future. You will learn how to help the appraisee reach desirable standards, such as through a personal development plan. You should learn about career planning so that you are in a position to advise the appraisee on how to equip themselves for opportunities that may arise in the future. As an appraisee, you will learn how to listen, be assertive about your learning and development needs, ask questions, and accept feedback.

- **Discipline**. If an employee breaches a rule or consistently fails to reach the required level of job performance, then a disciplinary situation may arise. Unfortunately, from time to time you may have to discipline staff. There is a correct approach to discipline, which should be learned. You will learn about the shortcomings of human nature and how to be firm but fair in your approach. You will learn the importance of establishing the facts and not be influenced by opinion, assumptions or prejudice. You will need to be familiar with the disciplinary code in your company and employment legislation. You will probably acquire experience of dealing with trade union officials such as shop stewards.

- **Conflict resolution**. This is the process by which disputes occur and are resolved. The usual parties to disputes in a company are unions or staff associations and management. The distribution of budgetary resources may be a source of conflict between competing managers. Good personnel policies and procedures in areas like grievances, disciplining, arbitration and conciliation will eliminate possible sources of conflict. Fair and imaginative sharing of budgetary resources will reduce a possible source of conflict. As a manager, you will learn how to identify the source of conflict, develop creative solutions and resolve problems using a win–win approach. You will need to learn excellent interpersonal relationship skills in the process. You will learn about negotiation and arbitration procedures and how to behave sensitively in delicate situations.

On-the-Job Learning: Staff Development

- **Coaching**. One of the key duties of managers is to coach staff to improve their on-the-job performance. Coaching is where you give instruction to staff to maintain or improve work performance. From a manager's perspective, the best way to learn is to coach. Coaching is the way that the knowledge, skills, attitude, experience and wisdom of a manager can be passed on to a staff member. To coach effectively you must think through the skills you want to pass on and how the learning process can best be facilitated. You must know how adults learn and their different learning styles and the best way to facilitate learning. Coaching works on the principle that you help people learn, but you cannot teach them. Listening, asking questions, demonstrating, testing understanding and empathising are some of the skills involved in coaching. You must also learn which coaching style is appropriate to your particular situation. Avail of any opportunity to get formal training in coaching skills.

- **Mentoring**. Mentoring is a relationship between a mentor and a mentoree where the mentor facilitates the learning and development of the mentoree. Mentoring differs from coaching in that mentoring is general rather than specific, is long-term rather than short-term in focus and is delivered by someone other than the line manager. Mentoring is a great opportunity to help someone else reach their potential while at the same time developing a whole range of skills. You will develop counselling, listening, questioning and empathy skills in establishing and maintaining the relationship with the mentoree. You will learn how adults learn and their different learning styles and how to develop other people. You will learn how to be facilitative and objective rather than directive and partisan in your mentoring relationship. You will develop creative problem-solving skills by facilitating the mentoree to generate alternative and novel solutions for consideration. You will develop influencing and negotiation skills in your dealings with senior management on behalf of the mentoree.

- **Counselling**. Counselling has been defined as the process of helping others help themselves. In the process, we gain a better understanding of human nature and of ourselves. Managers are expected to counsel their staff from time to time. Life events such as bereavement, ill health and mid-life crises will give you ample opportunity to practise your skills. It is a great opportunity for a manager to develop good counselling skills. These include reflective listening, empathy, sensitivity and facilitation skills. The communication style used in counselling is non-directive and facilitates open discussion. In general, adopt an approach of reflective listening, paraphrasing and summarising. You should develop an attitude of empathy, genuineness and unconditional positive regard. In career counselling, you may help staff to assess their values, define challenges they face and set their goals. You may help staff identify the opportunities available to them and recognise their unique strengths. On the other hand, being counselled by a senior manager can help us to develop our resources and opportunities for growth.

- **Facilitating**. These days, managers should be facilitators rather than directors. Make suggestions rather than offer advice and be there as a resource when needed. As a facilitator, you will need to develop good analytical and diagnostic skills, excellent communication skills, be able to deal with conflict and emotional issues and encourage others to come up with a wide range of options.

- **Delegation**. Delegation is a normal aspect of successful management. A manager gets work done through other people, so delegation is an essential part of the job. Delegation is the process where a manager gives some of his or her work to one or more staff members to do. Delegation is not abdication. Managers retain responsibility for the work done and should make the staff member accountable to them for the correct performance of the work delegated. It is important that the person to whom the work is delegated has the experience, capacity, willingness and expertise to do the work. The work should be of such a standard as to stretch and offer challenge. Delegation provides a great opportunity for staff to learn and develop themselves. From the manager's viewpoint, it is also a great learning opportunity. The manager learns how to set objectives; to set standards of performance expected; to allocate sufficient resources and authority to get the job done; to control so that progress is checked and quality maintained; to trust and let go and give the person freedom to do the job; and to train, counsel and coach as the need arises. Work may also be delegated to the manager from his or her senior manager. This will be a great learning and development opportunity for the manager and an opportunity to display his or her ability to get things done.

On-the-Job Learning Models

The CRAMP model, which was evolved by the Industrial Training Research Unit Ltd., covers the type of skills that most of us need to develop for learning on-the-job. CRAMP stands for:

CRAMP MODEL

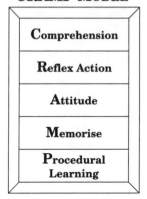

- **Comprehension**. Your understanding of how business works and how the economy operates. In particular, how your department interfaces with the other departments within the company and how the company interfaces with other competitors in the industry. These skills underlie decision-making and problem-solving.

- **Reflex action**. The acquisition of skilled movements and perceptual abilities. The skill, speed and dexterity with which you do job tasks. Keyboarding skills are a good example.

- **Attitude**. You need to become aware of the particular culture of the company. This will be reflected in the way that it conducts business, treats customers and staff. Personally, a positive attitude will be reflected in the excellence of the service you provide.

- **Memorise**. You will need to memorise the names of people in other departments that you have dealings with, branches or other companies within the organisation, as well as codes, prices, safety regulations and company rules.

- **Procedural learning**. You need to know how the policies, systems and procedures in the company operate. This will enable you to do your job more efficiently and effectively.

A similar type model is called KASH. This stands for:

KASH MODEL

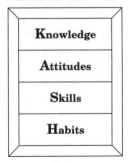

Knowledge

A few useful principles here are:

- The more meaningful the knowledge, the more easily it can be learned.

- Knowledge is learned faster when it is made distinctive. When studying, for example, highlighting a passage with a highlighter pen or underlining a difficult passage in your notes in red makes the passage distinctive and easier to learn.

Attitudes

A positive mental attitude is essential if you want to be a successful learner. Successful learners adopt the following attitudes:

- They display a positive can-do attitude. They see possibilities for learning rather than constraints. There is no failure, only feedback. Thus they see problems as challenges to be overcome and mistakes as learning opportunities.

- They have high expectations about successful learning outcomes and thus their success as learners becomes a self-fulfilling prophecy.

- They are open to new learning opportunities and believe in the concept of lifelong learning, continuous self-development and improvement.

- They are aware that the subconscious mind can't tell the difference between a real experience and one that is vividly imagined.

Thus they realise that it is possible to programme the mind for successful learning.

- They articulate, visualise and emotionalise their learning affirmations, which are in the present tense, personal, clear, specific and positive.

- They surround themselves with like-minded people who believe in self-development and lifelong learning.

- They immerse themselves in a world of self-improvement books, tapes, videos and course programmes.

- They find learning inherently satisfying.

Skill

Psychologists have found that the best way to learn skills is to follow the following guidelines:

- Work in short practice sessions spaced widely apart, instead of longer sessions held closer together.

- One of the best ways to learn tasks is to imitate experts.

- There is no substitute for doing it yourself, rather than watching someone else do it.

- You learn better if you get immediate feedback on your performance.

- Practise difficult parts of a task separately and then try to incorporate them into the task as a whole.

Habits

A habit is something you learn to do over and over again without thinking about it. Many of the actions we perform every day are habits. Imagine how time-consuming it would be to tie your shoelace every day if you had to think about the precise movements involved. A habit is different than an instinct. An instinct is inborn, rather than learned. When we learn, we connect a stimulus and a response that did not exist before, thus forming a habit. Many psychologists believe that:

- People will learn a habit only if it benefits them. This is called a reward or reinforcement. If they feel good about the habit, they tend to keep it.

- If a habit offers no reward or is unpleasant, people generally will discard it. Thus habitual smokers enjoy smoking and are reluctant to give them up, despite the risks to health involved. The immediate pleasure is stronger than the distant possibility of illness. However, smokers who suffer a heart attack usually are only too willing to give up smoking on doctor's orders in the expectation that it will prolong their lives.

- In an experiment, psychologists taught rats habits and then cut their nervous systems at many points. Despite the cuts, the rats continued to perform the habits. This suggests that the learning of habits does not depend on specific nerve connections and does not occur only in particular parts of the brain.

The Process of Learning a Skill

This can be recalled by the mnemonic SAILORS:

- **See** yourself using the skill. Visualise what it will feel like to have acquired the skill. See yourself becoming more and more proficient. Think about your motivation and commitment to learn the skill.

- **Aim** for a target time in which to acquire the skill and level of expertise sought. The target should be realistic and should be broken down into sub-targets.

- **Imitate** a model of proficiency which you admire.

- **Look** for the special skills of your model.

- **Opportunities** to practise must be created. Practice must be planned and regular if proficiency is to be achieved. Skill development takes time and persistence. Practice makes perfect and practice makes permanent.

- **Reflect** on your performance and look for feedback. Ask your model for feedback.

- **Support**. Seek out sources of support to keep you motivated and on track. The flat parts of the learning curve are the times when you may need encouragement and a helping hand. In some organisations, mentors may take on this role.

Summary

LAYGO stands for learn as you go. Some of the approaches discussed were:

- Self-directed learning
- Self-reflection
- Learning from your mistakes
- Continuous improvement
- Career development
- Action learning
- Just-in-time learning.

On-the-job learning techniques include the following:

- Groups:
  - ◆ Project or task force
  - ◆ Meetings
  - ◆ Committee work
- Personal development:
  - ◆ Job rotation
  - ◆ Social occasions
  - ◆ Tasks
- Benchmarking:
  - ◆ Modelling
  - ◆ Visits to customers, suppliers and competitors
  - ◆ Work shadowing

- Demanding work:
  - ◆ Deputising
  - ◆ Promotion
  - ◆ Job enrichment and job enlargement
  - ◆ Budgeting
- Communications skills:
  - ◆ Briefing and debriefing
  - ◆ Negotiation
  - ◆ Interviewing and appraisal
  - ◆ Discipline and conflict resolution
- Staff development:
  - ◆ Coaching and mentoring
  - ◆ Counselling and facilitating
  - ◆ Delegation

CRAMP, an on-the-job learning model, was discussed. CRAMP stands for:

- **C**omprehension
- **R**eflex action
- **A**ttitude
- **M**emorise
- **P**rocedural learning.

KASH is a mnemonic which stands for:

- **K**nowledge
- **A**ttitude
- **S**kill
- **H**abits

The process of learning a skill can be recalled by the mnemonic SAILORS:

- **See** yourself using the skill
- **A**im for target
- **I**mitate a model
- **L**ook for special skills
- **O**pportunities to practise
- **R**eflect
- **S**upport.

CHAPTER 10 LEARNING MAP

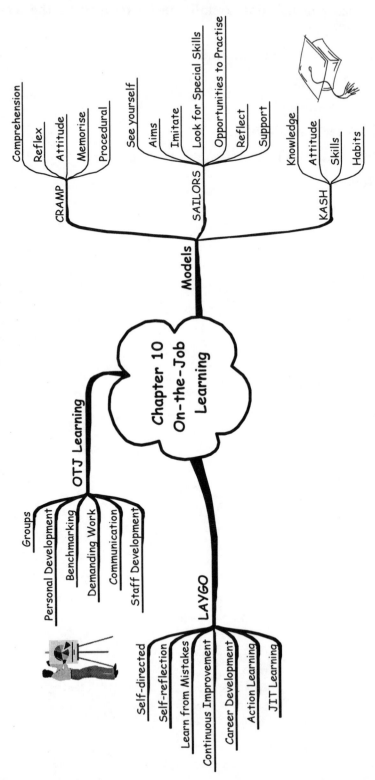

11

Off-the-Job Learning

"Anyone who stops learning is old, whether at twenty or eighty. Anyone who keeps learning stays young. The greatest thing in life is to keep your mind young."
— Henry Ford

♦ *What is the difference between training and development?*

♦ *How can I develop myself through academic courses?*

♦ *How can I develop useful skills in outside bodies?*

♦ *What are the techniques of off-the-job learning?*

♦ *What is an assessment centre?*

♦ *What is a corporate learning centre?*

Training and Development

Training is about acquiring new skills, improving your existing skills and learning about new technology. Development is about lifelong learning, preparation for promotion and career advancement. A good personal development plan will consist of both on-the-job and off-the-job learning. Off-the-job learning is particularly suitable for conceptual learning, keeping up-to-date and broadening the range of your knowledge and skills. Roger Ascham said in 1570:

> Learning teacheth more in one year than experience in twenty, and learning teacheth safely, when experience maketh more miserable than wise . . . It is costly wisdom that is bought by experience."

So the best learning is acquired through a combination of on-the-job and off-the-job experiences.

Academic Opportunities

There are now a wide range of programmes you can undertake on a part-time basis while holding down your daytime job. These range from one-year certificate programmes right up to doctorate level, which may take up to six years part-time. The following are some of the opportunities:

- Certificates

- Diplomas

- Degrees

- Postgraduate

- Professional qualifications

- Part-time distance learning and Open University programmes.

Short Courses

These may be run by your own internal training and development department or by outside training consultants. These range from one-day programmes to one week or longer. The longer programmes may be in modular form spread over several months. The modern trend is for the certification of programmes. Short courses may take the form of:

- **Conferences**. A conference is a group of people from the same organisation or different organisations who come together to discuss and explore issues of common concern. Problem identification and solution is often the objective of a conference. However, the conference is also used to exchange information and to improve co-operation. You will meet people from different organisations with different experiences and perspectives. Conferences are also a great source for networking opportunities. Many professional bodies hold annual conferences to update their members.

- **Workshops**. A workshop is a group of people with a common interest or problem who meet to improve their proficiency or understanding of a subject by study, research and discussion. There is great flexibility, with help being provided within groups, between groups and by the facilitator. The learning situations tend to be based on interests and needs identified by the participants themselves, rather than by experts. Workshops provide an excellent opportunity to learn from others with different backgrounds.

- **Seminars**. A seminar has been defined as a short course making extensive use of participating methods and devoted to the exclusive study of one subject with the aim of furthering knowledge in that area. It may be facilitated by an expert. Like conferences and workshops, seminars provide a great opportunity to exchange views, learn from other people's diverse experience and make contacts.

Involvement in Outside Bodies

This is usually done on a voluntary basis, but may provide marvellous opportunities for gaining experience in roles which you would not normally perform at work. Opportunities for learning include acting as the president, secretary, treasurer, public relations officer, education officer or membership officer. Some of these jobs may have a high profile, so that you may get experience dealing with the media, liaising with other organisations, organising conferences and chairing meetings. They will give you an opportunity to develop your interpersonal relationship skills in formal and social situations. The various bodies might be of the following types:

- Professional

- Trade

- Cultural

- Charities

- Social

- Recreational.

Off-the-Job Learning: Groups

There are a wide range of off-the-job training approaches. The following are some of the best known:

- **Outdoor experiential training (OET)**. This is where a group of managers engage in challenging outdoor activities, such as hill climbing, water rafting or tree climbing to learn about their personal styles of interaction and tolerance limits, in order to improve their ability to get along with other people. One particular goal of OET is to eliminate behaviours typical to a manager's role at work. Consequently, while on the programme, participants are expected to avoid formal dress, the use of titles, or any signs of deference which they may enjoy in their own organisation. During the OET, which can last from one to five days, social barriers are broken down and managers get to know each other as individuals rather than as roles or titles. The leadership qualities of participants often come to the fore. Some research suggests that groups who participate in OET are more cohesive and effective for several months after the experience.

- **Business games**. These can be used to simulate the functional departments of a business and how they interact to achieve corporate goals. Players may take on the roles of functional managers and may be constrained to operate within financial budgets and other limited resources. Teams may compete against other teams representing other companies. The complexity of modern business can be simulated by the computer and so business games have taken on a new reality. The effect of strategies, actions and decisions can be fed back to participants in the management game. Business games may be used to teach strategy and planning skills, functional skills such as marketing and finance, and human behaviour skills such as leadership and communications. The lessons learned in a business game may be transferred to a business.

- **Junior boards**. These may be set up to shadow the board of directors in order to give younger managers some insight in how the company is governed, how decisions are made and how policies are formulated. The junior board learns how to take a strategic view of the business. They may be given the same information on which to base their decisions as the senior board. The decisions the junior board would have taken can be benchmarked against the actual decisions taken by the board. The main purpose of the junior board is to develop rising stars for future senior management positions within the company. Because they have no real power, responsibility or accountability, this method of developing managers is not widely used.

- **T-groups**. These are also known as sensitivity training. T-groups focus on improving communication between individuals. This is training led by a facilitator with the intention of fostering changes in attitudes and behaviour necessary to improve interpersonal relationship skills. The idea is to get feedback on how others perceive and feel about your behaviour. Through discussion in the group, with the help of the facilitator, participants would change to more effective, more rewarding interpersonal behaviours and the new patterns of behaviour would be reinforced. The ability to relate well to other people is possibly the most important skill to a successful management career.

- **Role-play** is a type of simulation, a type of acting. Role players may operate to a script or may act to general guidelines and ad lib. The aim is to give people a taste of the real thing. Managers learn by doing. In management training, it may be used to develop interpersonal skills such as negotiation, interviewing, customer relations, conflict resolution and so on. Role-playing is also frequently used to change attitudes through "role reversal". This is where managers change roles to develop new perspectives. For example, in a negotiation role-play, the manager may play the role of the employer and then play the role of the trade union official. It is a good way of learning empathy skills, as to do it effectively you need to take on the persona of the role.

Off-the-Job Learning: Thinking

- **Reflection**, including mental rehearsal. Reflection is the second stage of the learning cycle of "do something, think about it, conclude and then do something differently". Thinking is probably the hardest thing that you do and that is why so few people do it. Mental rehearsal is a type of prospective learning. You might mentally rehearse a presentation that you will be giving to the senior management team in the near future. Psychologists maintain that mental rehearsal is nearly as effective as doing the real thing. Mental rehearsal is a proactive activity. You are thinking ahead and anticipating any problems that may arise. You can then put contingency plans in place to cater for these problems if they happen.

- **Listening**. The reason we have two ears and one mouth is because we should listen twice as much as we speak. Good managers should be good listeners. Most of us are so preoccupied with our own thoughts that even when we are supposed to be listening we are only rehearsing what we are about to say next. Good listening skills are demanded of managers in interviewing, counselling, coaching, mentoring and handling grievances.

- **Observing**. The police are trained to observe and some policemen often develop great powers of observation. Most of the rest of us go around with our eyes shut. In business organisation, people are trained to be observant and develop an eye for improvements in methods and procedures. The eyes are our greatest sense for learning. We should take a leaf from the great scientists of history and observe what's going on around us in a questioning way.

Off-the-Job Learning: Personal Development

- **Secondment**. This is where a manager goes to another organisation to gain experience and further development. Secondment should be used as part of a planned management development programme. A civil servant may be seconded to a commercial organisation to learn how a business operates in a competitive environment. On the other hand, a manager in the commercial sector may be seconded to a civil service department to find out how government departments operate. It provides a unique opportunity for managers to operate in a new environment, experience a different company culture, and learn new perspectives, systems and procedures. You learn how to make decisions based on your own judgement and experience. You also extend your network of business contacts. A manager moving from a large to a small company often learns to become more self-reliant, as the same back-up and support facilities are not available. When the person on secondment comes back, they should be debriefed by their manager on what they learned and how they propose to apply this learning to their own organisation.

- **Sabbaticals** or career breaks are often used to give managers an opportunity to pursue an outside interest. For example, you may wish to take a year off to write the book that you always intended to write but never seemed to have the time for. It enables managers to leave a job and subsequently return after an agreed period of absence. It is important that re-entry is guaranteed at the same level. Sometimes a change is better than a rest and sabbaticals may revitalise a manager's interest in a career that has become stale and stagnant.

- **Public speaking**. Managers are called upon from time to time to make presentations to staff, colleagues and senior management. It is unlikely that you will progress to senior management positions without the ability to make good presentations. Therefore it is in your own interest to take every opportunity to develop good presentation skills. Go on a presentation skills programme. Volunteer your services to the training and development department, who are always looking for speakers on their training programmes. You could build a presentation around your functional expertise and knowledge and show how it relates to the rest of the organisation.

- **External mentoring**. You might get the opportunity to mentor people outside the company during your own spare time. This gives you the chance to develop the same mentoring skills needed as if you were doing it for your own company. You will need to develop interpersonal skills including counselling, listening, questioning and empathy to establish and maintain a relationship with a mentoree. You will need to understand how adults learn and have the ability to guide and develop people.

You will need to develop facilitation skills and be able to influence and negotiate with senior management. You will also get a very good insight into how other company cultures operate.

- **Reading** is a great way of self-development. Many people stop reading serious books after their formal education. Most people that buy serious books never get beyond the first few pages. Most managers' reading consists of just glancing through business magazines or professional journals. Many companies circulate these with most managers just ticking the circulation list and passing it on. This is a pity, because there is a big world out there waiting to be discovered and you can pick up useful ideas by reading widely in your discipline. Identify the areas in which you need to build up information and expertise. You should draw up a reading plan of books to meet your management development needs. Set yourself the target of reading two management books a month. In a year, you will have read 24! Reading can broaden your horizons by proxy in a way that would be impossible in a normal lifetime of experiences.

- **Management by wandering about (MBWA)**. How many managers lock themselves away each day in their office and are seldom seen again? MBWA is about wandering about purposely to keep in touch with employees and the problems they encounter on the shop floor. If you are a familiar figure on the shop floor, staff will tell you things that you wouldn't normally hear if you were depending solely on the formal channels of communication. MBWA shows you are human, accessible and concerned about your employees and interested in what is going on.

Off-the-Job Learning: Resolving Issues

- **Problem-solving**. As a manager, anything that will help you solve problems better should be learned. Various conceptual models in management will also help you solve problems better. The greater the range of problem-solving techniques in your management armoury the better.

- **Decision-making**. Our lives are determined by the decisions
  we make and by the decisions others make for us. The ability to
  make good decisions is critical to a successful management career. There is a widespread belief that we can all learn to make
  better decisions. The rational approach to decision-making as-
  sumes a logical, linear set of steps. It includes defining the
  problem, collecting information, analysing it, considering alternatives, making a choice, implementing it and then checking to
  see if it worked. This approach is very useful as a model, but in
  practice few managers follow it. Decisions are often influenced
  by feelings, intuition, experience and perceived outcomes. Outcomes include being aware of the consequences of making a bad
  decision. Being given responsibility early in your career for a
  significant aspect of the business is essential if you wish to progress to a senior management position. This gives you the opportunity to make decisions and learn from experience. The
  more decisions you make, the easier decision-making becomes
  and the better you become at making decisions. Managers are
  often evaluated by the effectiveness of their decisions.

- **Questioning** is probably one of the best ways of learning.
  Questions provide a sense of purpose. They focus our concentration. One of the most effective ways of learning is seeking out
  answers to questions that you have posed to yourself. A curious
  mind is like a magnet drawing the answers towards it. For personal development, the most productive questions are those
  which stimulate fresh ideas and insights rather than address
  the familiar. Questions can help you identify a problem, generate alternatives, make choices, discover new information and
  see things from different perspectives. You can find out anything provided you ask the right questions.

- **Case studies**. Case studies offer a less costly alternative to
  simulations, often with equal learning benefits. They provide a
  great vehicle for the development and exercise of problem-
  solving skills. Managers study a written narrative of an actual
  or fictitious organisation. The case may include the history of
  the organisation, the key management players, financial information, market information and competition. They devise a so-

lution based on assumptions about resources, economic and legal constraints, and develop an implementation plan. Case studies can be studied individually or in groups. It is important that feedback on the manager's solution and implementation plan is provided so that successful transfer of training can occur to the work situation. Case studies are an important aspect of MBA programmes and other business degrees.

Off-the-Job Learning: Training

- **Demonstrations**. This is where the manager gives a live demonstration of a task, skill or procedure accompanied by an explanation. The purpose is to provide a model and some practice for staff before they do it themselves. To be a good demonstrator, you must be competent in the technique of demonstration, know how people learn, know how to explain things clearly, have a friendly but directive teaching style, know how to handle questions, and know how to analyse participants' problems and provide feedback. A manager will learn how to break down a task into logical steps and how to present them in a clear and understandable way.

- **In-tray exercises**. These may be used in management training. The in-tray simulates a typical day's work in the form of letters, memos, reports, fax, e-mail and diary notes, which need to be dealt with by the manager. The exercise can be made more realistic by including interruptions in the form of telephone calls, personal calls, urgent meetings, discipline problems and so on. In-tray exercises test the manager's ability to solve problems, work under pressure and prioritise tasks as in the real world. In-tray exercises are an integral part of the assessment centre approach.

- **Simulations**. These are learning activities designed to replicate the real world situation. A well-designed simulation can provide more efficient and effective training than the use of the actual equipment. Best-known examples include business games, flight simulators, driving simulators and power station operation simulators. Police officers learn "seek and search" techniques in simulated streets and houses. Soldiers learn how to fire missiles in simulated conditions. Bank officials learn cashier techniques at simulated counters. Multimedia courseware enables employees to explore safely the operation of expensive and potentially dangerous equipment in a risk-free environment. Modern computer technology now enables the creation of "virtual reality" such as simulated surgery and is creating extraordinary opportunities for the use of simulation. Expert systems are computer programs that mimic expertise in a particular area of knowledge such as medicine or taxation.

Assessment Centres

These combine in-tray exercises, role-play, case studies, diagnostic analysis, simulations, group discussion, group tasks and interviews. Psychometric tests may be used to help managers identify strengths and weaknesses in behavioural areas. Assessment centres may be used for selection, placement, identification of potential, promotion, management development and training. Although sometimes used for judging potential, the assessment centre can be more productively used to identify the development needs of managers and may be called a development centre. Managers will be more inclined to use a development centre if it is not used for assessment or evaluation of management potential.

As a development centre, it can be used to help managers develop their career plans. In other words, it will help managers identify their development needs, draw up learning objectives, design personal development plans, monitor progress and identify their learning styles. Managers are helped to clarify their strengths and identify any weaknesses that need to be addressed. Participants may be offered further training and development or assigned a mentor to support their subsequent development.

Corporate Learning Centres

A corporate learning centre is a place within a company which provides learning resources for staff training and development. It is a tangible resource to meet the lifelong learning needs of staff. Corporate learning centre courses make learning accessible, easy, self-paced and interesting. The courses are designed around different forms of media. They range from text-based, audio and videotapes to CD-ROM and Internet. However, unlike teacher-centred conventional learning, the responsibility for the learning is solely with the learner. The following are the usual learning resources in a corporate learning centre:

- **Text-based course materials**. These may include course programme notes donated by staff, correspondence course material or manuals containing human resource development material and exercises.

- **Books**. Depending on the needs of the particular organisation, a wide range of books including management, information technology and engineering may be stocked. The centre may operate a library system giving books out on loan to staff.

- **Videos** are available covering all aspects of business. These may be viewed in the centre or loaned out to staff to be viewed at home.

- **Audios** now cover all areas of business. The big advantage of audio is that you can listen to them while driving or stuck in traffic jams. You might cover the equivalent of a university course in a year or two while commuting to and from work — a much more productive use of your time.

- **CD-ROM**. Every aspect of business is now available on CD-ROM. You can teach yourself anything through this medium. All aspects of computer skills and management skills are available.

Summary

There are a wide range of opportunities for management development off-the-job, including academic courses, short training courses and involvement in outside bodies such as professional institutes and charities.

The following off-the-job management training and development techniques were discussed:

- Groups
  - Outdoor experiential training
  - Business games
  - Junior boards
  - T-groups
  - Role play
- Thinking
  - Reflection
  - Listening
  - Observing
- Personal Development
  - Secondment
  - Sabbaticals
  - Public speaking
  - External mentoring
  - Reading
  - MBWA
- Resolving Issues
  - Problem-solving
  - Decision-making
  - Questioning
  - Case studies
- Training
  - Demonstrations
  - In-tray exercises
  - Simulations

The role of assessment centres and corporate learning centres in management development were discussed.

CHAPTER 11 LEARNING MAP

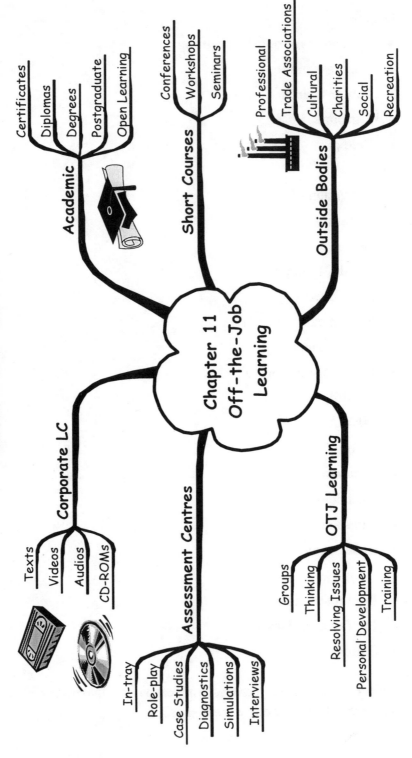

Bibliography

Armstrong, Michael (1993), *A Handbook of Personnel Management Practice*, London: Kogan Page.

Braham, Barbara J. (1995), *Creating a Learning Organisation*, London: Kogan Page.

Burgoyne, John (1999), *Developing Yourself, Your Career and Your Organisation*, London: Lemos & Crane.

Cole, G.A. (1995), *Management Theory and Practice*, Fourth Edition, London: DP Publications.

Conlan, Roberta (1999), *States of Mind: New Discoveries about How Our Brain Makes Us Who We Are*, New York: John Wiley & Sons.

DePorter, Bobbi (1998), *Quantum Learning for Business*, London: Piatkus.

DePorter, Bobbi and Mike Hernacki (1993), *Quantum Learning: Unleash the Genius Within You*, London: Piatkus.

Gardner, Howard (1997), *Extraordinary Minds*, London: Weidenfeld & Nicholson.

Gardner, Howard (1993), *Frames of Mind: The Theory of Multiple Intelligences*, London: Fontana.

Goleman, Daniel (1995), *Emotional Intelligence*, London: Bloomsbury.

Hansen, K.J. and R.C. Waterman (1966), "Evaluation of Research in Business Education", *National Business Education Quarterly*, Volume 35, pp. 81–84.

Harrison, Rosemary (1992), *Employee Development*, London: Institute of Personnel Management.

Hooper, Judith and Dick Teresi (1986), *The Three-Pound Universe*, New York: Macmillan Publishing Company.

Honey, Peter (1994), *101 Ways to Develop Your People Without Really Trying: A Manager's Guide to Work-based Learning*, Berkshire: Published by Dr. Peter Honey.

Honey, Peter and Alan Mumford (1986), *Using Your Learning Styles*, Berkshire: Published by Dr. Peter Honey.

Kirkpatrick, D.L. (1976), *Evaluation of Training*, Training and Development Handbook, New York: McGraw-Hill.

Malone, Samuel A. (1997), *Mind Skills for Managers*, Aldershot: Gower.

Malone, Samuel A. (1997), *How to Set Up and Manage a Corporate Learning Centre*, Aldershot: Gower.

Malone, Samuel A. (1996), *Learning to Learn*, London: CIMA.

Malone, Samuel A. (1999), *Success Skills for Managers*, Dublin: Oak Tree Press.

Malone, Samuel A. (1995), "A Critical Evaluation of Mind Maps in an Adult Learning Environment", unpublished thesis, University of Sheffield.

Mumford, Alan (1993), *How Managers Can Develop Managers*, Aldershot: Gower.

Mumford, Alan (1997), *Management Development Strategies for Action*, Third Edition, London: Institute of Personnel and Development.

Megginson, David and Vivian Whitaker (1996), *Cultivating Self-Development*, London: Institute of Personnel and Development.

Pedler, Mike and Tom Boydell (1999), *Managing Yourself*, London: Lemos & Crane.

Robertson, Ian H. (1999), *Mind Sculpture: Your Brain's Untapped Potential*, London: Bantam Press.

Rupp, Rebecca (1998), *Committed to Memory: How We Remember and Why We Forget*, London: Aurum Press Ltd.

Saunders, Mark, Philip Lewis and Adrian Thornhill (1997), *Research Methods for Business Students*, London: Pitman Publishing.

Smither, Robert D., John M. Houston and Sandra D. McIntire (1996), *Organisation Development: Strategies for Changing Environments*, New York: HarperCollins Publishers.

Waters, Michael (1996), *The Dictionary of Personal Development*, Shaftesbury: Element Books Ltd.

Index